Susie Cooper

AN ELEGANT AFFAIR

BRYN YOUDS

Specially commissioned photography by
EARL BEESLEY

THAMES AND HUDSON

For Jill

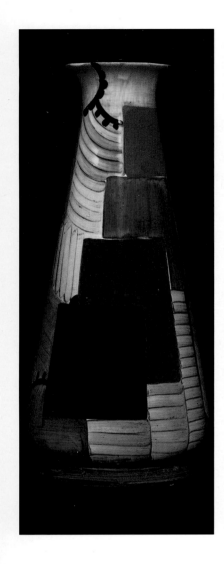

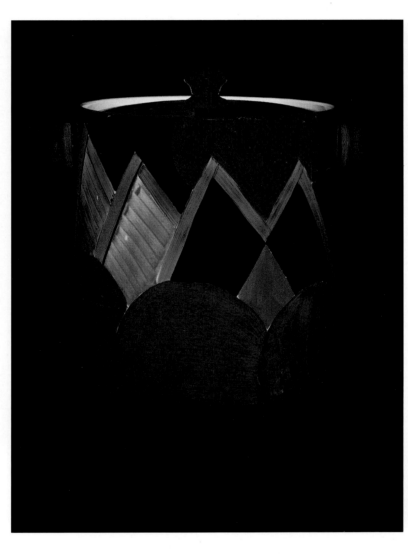

This page Geometric designs of the Art Deco period: 'Cubist' bottle vase, 'Moon and Mountains' biscuit barrel and casket.

Title page illustration
The 'Leaping Deer' table centre, made in 1937 at the request of Gene Fondeville, Susie Cooper's agent in New York. The colouring was designed to complement a range of wash-banded dinner-ware.

© 1996   Thames and Hudson Ltd, London

Text © 1996 Bryn Youds
Special photography © Earl Beesley

First published in the United States of America in 1996 by
Thames and Hudson Inc., 500 Fifth Avenue, New York, New York 10110

Library of Congress Catalog Card Number 96-60054

ISBN 0-500-27888-1

Printed in Hong Kong

CONTENTS

A range of Susie Cooper coffee cups (*opposite*), from top left to top right: E478, 1528, 'Elegance' 1707, 1526, 'Seagull' 857, 1483, 1467, 1382, 654, E137, E282, 1101, E219, E199, 1958, E213, 1485, E171, 500, 1971, E484, 933. Reference numbers are those in the Susie Cooper Productions Earthenware Pattern Book.

Susie Cooper had intended to write the foreword to this book. Unfortunately, this was not possible before her death at the age of ninety-two. However, she had already told me what she hoped the book would be like and what effect it would have. She dearly hoped that it would show people how her work had evolved but, above all, that it would inspire students of design to experiment and to follow their personal ambitions. When I said that I wanted the book to be a source of inspiration for all those who saw it, she replied, 'Yes, I think that would be very nice'. This book, then, is specially dedicated to the memory of Susie Cooper and to all those who find inspiration in her work.

Susie Cooper is a name synonymous with excellence in ceramic design; she was without question one of the most important and most prolific of all British designers. She set the highest standards for quality and innovation for over seventy years, and many of her works are icons of ceramic design. Her work, indeed, provides us with a mirror of design history in the twentieth century, while her vision, her uncompromising approach to design and her experimental methods point the way forward for the next century.

It is hoped that this book will provide enjoyment for those who are exploring the work of Susie Cooper for the first time, as well as for those who have had long experience of her ceramics. The brilliant designs illustrated here should also provide inspiration for students of art and design, proof that work can be produced which is both critically and publicly acclaimed and that careers can be built in the face of adversity. Susie Cooper's professional life demonstrated the value of hard work and of strength of conviction. Above all, her work was informed by the pursuit of perfection.

Her ceramic designs have always been appreciated for their beauty and usefulness; they have now become much sought after by galleries and an enthusiastic band of collectors. The appeal of Susie Cooper's wares is their universality: there is something for everyone. The range of her work is awe-inspiring: eight decades of production from classics of Art Deco to breathtakingly simple polka dots and banding, quirky and intelligent adult and children's nursery wares, and astonishing floral patterns. Some of the work reproduced in this book has never before been seen in public; this includes not only ceramic designs but also textiles, paintings and sculpture.

Floral designs c. 1931–32 (*below*): cruet E470, preserve pot E207 and jug E389.

There is a purity in Susie Cooper's works which sprang from the desire to produce something both beautiful and useful. Even the most seemingly mundane of floral designs can, on close scrutiny, be seen to be of supreme accomplishment and economy, the qualities which Susie Cooper has indelibly stamped on twentieth-century ceramics.

CHAPTER ONE

These early figures (*opposite left* and *right*), 'Crouching Woman' and 'Spanish Dancer', were modelled by Susie Cooper in earthenware while she was still at Burslem School of Art.

PROLOGUE

1902-23

Susie Cooper was born Susan Vera Cooper in the Stansfield area of Burslem, Stoke-on-Trent, on 29 October 1902. The family was reasonably well-off, with a range of properties and business interests. These included a bakery, a grocery and a butcher's. There was also a family farm, which introduced to Susie at the earliest age a wealth of animal and nature subjects, providing her with subject-matter for the rest of her working life. When Susie painted a wood panel for her son's nursery forty years later, it was as if she were passing on her own childhood memories; simple drawings of young men and women working among quirkily caricatured animals are bathed in a nostalgic glow; in one corner a couple are courting, in another a man rests in the late summer sunshine.

Drawing was a keen interest of Susie Cooper as a child; family members recalled the young Susie sitting quietly hour after hour, making drawings from fashion plates in the elegant *Nash's Magazine*. Susie later admitted that, as a child, she could always be kept from mischief by being occupied with her pencils and water-colours.

As a child and young woman, Susie's work in the family bakery and grocery provided her with a valuable insight into the running of a business and a belief in the virtues of hard work. There, she found herself put to a multitude of tasks, from black-leading

The childhood memories of Susie Cooper were celebrated in this wood panel (*above*), which she painted for her son's nursery in the early nineteen-forties.

A group photograph (*below*) of the Cooper family taken about 1913; Susie is fourth from the left in the front row, standing just behind her mother.

stoves to putting the crosses on to hot-cross buns, as well as working behind the counter of the shop. To open up possibilities beyond the immediate concerns of the family businesses, Susie enrolled in an evening class in typing, but found that this was certainly not to her taste. Since no-one seemed particularly concerned about what the youngest of the seven Cooper children should do, Susie was able to follow her own inclinations and very quickly exchanged the typing course for drawing classes at the Burslem School of Art. The college records note her registration for the academic year 1919–20, age 16 years and 11 months, the fee seven shillings and sixpence. But this early art education was literally priceless; Susie's work in the 'freehand and plant form' classes was of a very high quality and at the end of the year she was offered a scholarship for a full-time programme starting in September 1920. It was invaluable, too, because of her introduction to Gordon Forsyth, the newly appointed 'Superintendent for Art Instruction in Stoke-on-Trent', who was to be a great influence on Susie.

Forsyth had been educated at the Royal College of Art, London, very much in the aftermath of the Arts and Crafts Movement. However, unlike some of the key inspirational figures, such as Ruskin and Morris, Forsyth was passionately pro-industry; that is, he advocated industrial production informed by good art and design. He first expressed this advocacy of the unity of crafts-

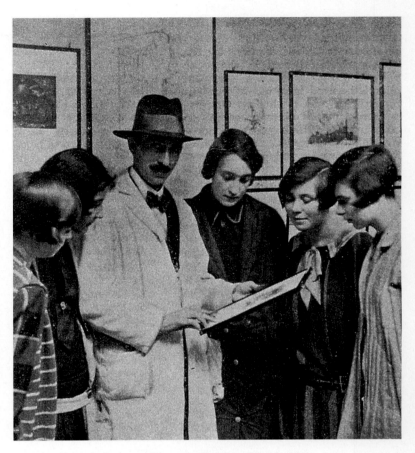

Gordon Forsyth during a visit to the Burslem School of Art.

manship and industry in his role as art director of Minton, Hollins and Co., tile manufacturers, before moving to the post of art director for the Pilkington Tile and Pottery Co. His lecture to the National Pottery Council in 1921 clearly anticipated the guiding values of Susie Cooper's approach to ceramic design and production: 'Art was always sound economy. It took the same amount of coal to fire bad work as good and it was the elimination of bad work and the waste of human endeavour that art stood for.'

Forsyth taught Susie to work directly and not to be too precious. Over-labouring a drawing, for example, would 'kill off the life in the work … just do it', she was told by Forsyth. This lesson was to prove especially useful in under-glaze ceramic painting, in which decoration, once applied, cannot be removed. Forsyth's influence on Susie Cooper also made itself felt in a less direct way. An exhibition of Pilkington wares at art school introduced her to the shimmering excitement of lustre pottery, an additional inspiration, and she began to think that she might like to produce such beautiful objects herself.

Susie turned her hand to a wide range of activities at the art school; wood-carving, for instance, was a particular interest. Other classes included stained-glass, with Forsyth himself, drawing from the antique, life class, freehand drawing and modelling. A number of her student water-colours and engravings survive, already clearly showing her polished design talents and analytical eye. Even her portraits from these early years show exceptional sensitivity.

Ironically, Susie's work in clay at the school was limited, though the handful of figures she did produce show very clearly her precocious and considerable modelling skills. It is perhaps significant that Susie received relatively little formal tutoring in ceramics; her concern to combine functionalism with artistic self-expression was developed very much in the work-place itself.

At first glance, these early figures display little of what we recognize as 'Susie Cooper design', but close examination does reveal early signs of her distinctive style. In the very first of her ceramic works, the 'Crouching Woman', the immediate impression is that of classical simplicity. The pose of the figure is the key element –

This powder bowl, crowned by a lady in crinoline, was made by Susie Cooper during her period at the Burslem School of Art.

Only two examples are known to exist of the 'Guin Yin' figure (*above*), modelled by Susie Cooper at the Burslem School of Art in slip-cast bone china.

The precocious talents of the young Susie Cooper are finely demonstrated in this water-colour (*right*) of a fellow student at Burslem School of Art.

graceful serenity is captured in the exquisite modelling; a particular sensitivity to form and the expression of that form is already apparent. The 'Spanish Dancer' is, in appearance, perhaps the most conventional of these figures, but it also contains clear early signs of her fastidious attention to detail. A swathe of frilled blue fabric clothes the figure, rippling to suggest the dancer's graceful steps. The gold brocade of the costume is painted in a flourish of stylized swirls and foliage, motifs which were to recur during her long career.

The 'Spanish Dancer' clearly illustrates Susie's interest in fashion and, while at the college, she formed the idea of taking up a career in the fashion industry. An application for a scholarship to the Royal College of Art to study fashion design was, however, rejected. It was the policy of the time to accept only candidates already working within industry. In order to fulfil this criterion Susie, on the advice of Gordon Forsyth, decided to take up a position at the local pottery firm of A. E. Gray and Co., Ltd., although it was considered rather less than desirable for a middle-class young woman to take a lowly position in a pottery factory. However, Gray's already employed Gordon Forsyth as a designer and so, keen to emulate her teacher, Susie began work. It was, incidentally, to be sixty-five years before Susie was accepted by the Royal College. In the meantime, the Burslem art school remained a focal point for Susie, both personally and professionally.

Two superb examples (*opposite*) of vase designs for A.E. Gray in the 'Gloria Lustre' range, pattern no. 5365, c. 1925.

THE DECO YEARS

1923–29

A.E. Gray and Co., Ltd. was a well-established and respected pottery decorating firm based in Hanley which was renowned for its modern designs. When Susie started work at Gray's in June 1922 she was surprised and more than a little upset, however, to find that a Miss Samuels had just been appointed designer. The appointment of Miss Samuels meant that, instead of designing, Susie was put to the relatively humble work of copying some of Gordon Forsyth's heraldic lions on to wares. Ceramics painted by Susie at this time are often marked with her initials and a small triangular symbol. One of the quirks of Gray's markings are stylish signatures and unusual symbols, known as 'rebuses', the meanings of which are unclear, although such inclusion of elaborate markings seems to emphasize the consciously artistic nature of Gray's pottery and particularly of the lustre pieces.

Susie's initiation into the pottery industry was at the basic level of piece-work paintress. This meant that payment was dependent upon the number of pieces a worker could decorate in a day. It was certainly hard work, but it was also important to her growing understanding of the business of decoration. Susie recounted later that, at first, she was unable to do banding, and so she had to pay another paintress out of her piece-work wage to finish the designs with a band. Unhappy with her unexpectedly lowly position, she eventually plucked up the courage to approach Edward Gray, the managing director, and tell him that she had come to work there to design. It was a well-timed complaint, as Miss Samuels was proving to be less than ideal in her role, and so Susie was appointed to assist her in the application of the designs on to the wares. The initial disappointments which Susie felt in her work with Gray's were soon dispelled as, within weeks, Miss Samuels left for the summer holidays and did not return. Susie was then elevated to the position of designer and set to work in her own studio office.

In 1923 Gordon Forsyth collaborated with Gray's on the introduction of a range of metallic lustre wares. The new pottery was given a specially designed back stamp of a sun ray and the title 'Gloria Lustre'. The products were clearly intended to enjoy a high profile within the company, and Susie set to work to expand the range. A selection of the sparkling lustre designs was shown at the the British Empire Exhibition of 1924 and the Paris Decorative Arts Exposition in 1925. These included fruit and floral patterns by Susie Cooper and Gray's won a silver medal. The Paris exhibition, the definitive showcase for Art Deco design, seems to have encouraged a greater degree of stylization in Susie Cooper's designs; even though she did not visit Paris, she nevertheless saw extensive coverage of the exhibits in the press. Indeed, during this period, contact with International Modernist ideas and imagery was beginning to influence her work. She had for years saved magazine cuttings of

Another example of 'Gloria Lustre' ware, with stylized floral design.

The Cooper family was gathered together again for the wedding of Agnes, Susie's sister, in 1927; this group photograph was taken outside the bungalow, 'Ben-i-Mora', which the sisters jointly owned.

More silver lustre design from the A.E. Gray period: the 'Persian Bird' coffee pot and associated 'Bird on Twig' designs.

designs and iconography which had especially struck her: the work of avant-garde designers and artists, notably of Picasso, featured strongly in her collection of clippings.

About 1925 Susie and her sister Agnes invested some of their hard-earned money in building a bungalow on a family plot of land at Baddiley Edge, just north of Stoke-on-Trent. Named 'Ben-i-Mora', the bungalow had hillside views and, most important, a basement studio incorporated into its modern design. As a little girl, Susie's niece remembers the excitement of the studio, with the huge pots of brushes and white ware for decorating lying in piles of packing straw. The fact that she obviously intended to work at home is further evidence of Susie's dedication to her career in the pottery industry and to her colossal appetite for hard work.

The limitations of lustre decoration rapidly became apparent to her; while spectacular on decorative items, the thin layer wore away very quickly on table-ware which had a practical use. The influx of bold, hand-painted floral wares from Czechoslovakia, coupled with the unsuitability of lustre decoration for practical use, led Susie to design more heavily in on-glaze enamels. She later calmly observed of the transition, 'I told Mr. Gray, if that is what people want, then that is what we must do.' Highly decorative designs of bold floral patterns now began to emerge in increasing numbers. In contrast to the imports with which they competed, these patterns often display the restrained elegance that was to become one of the key characteristics of Susie Cooper design.

The impact made at Gray's by Susie was soon boldly marked on the firm's pottery by a special back stamp with the message 'Designed by Susie Cooper'. The 'designer label' applied to the patterns produced by Susie certainly set a marketing trend within the Potteries; the names of Charlotte Rhead and Clarice Cliff were later added to the list of individually named designers to complete the trio of the 'ladies of the Potteries'.

Various forms in coloured lustre (*above*), designed by Susie Cooper for A.E. Gray.

A tea set (*right*) in Gray's hand-painted floral design of the nineteen-twenties, with pattern nos. 7956 (cup and saucer) and 7953 (bowl and dish). These lines of bold patterns were introduced specifically to compete with imports from Czechoslovakia.

A hand-painted vase (*above*) in the sumptuous colours of the Jazz Age – pattern 8099 designed by Susie Cooper for Gray's range of geometrically patterned ware.

Cooper's geometric designs, such as 'Cubist' and 'Moon and Mountains', seem to have been initiated in the latter part of the nineteen-twenties, although some reference is made to abstract designs in *The Pottery Gazette* report on Gray's output in 1926. It was not until 1928, however, that direct reference to the abstract patterns was made in the journal. Reporting on the British Industries Fair, the *Gazette* noted the presence of ware which was 'Cubist in type with blobs of colour, and streaks, with blues, greens and reds violently contrasted'.

The British Industries Fairs were crucial to the ceramics industry for sales of pottery at home and abroad and display was all-important. The traditional way of displaying pottery was to arrange the wares in dense groupings on row upon row of shelves. Susie, in her additional capacity as designer of the Gray's stands, asserted her modernist ideas of simplicity and restraint in strong, bold arrangements. Her co-ordination of decoration and her room-settings for the pottery displays attracted a great deal of attention, with no doubt resultant benefits to the sale of Gray's wares. Susie gave themes to her stands. In one instance, she adorned the display with deer and scrolling floral designs; in another, she utilized abstract designs on rolls of paper to complement the wares on display and even cushions on a sofa in the stand area were sewn by her to match the abstract patterns. She later recalled how these red triangular cushions had disturbed the representatives of Bass, the brewery company, since the red triangle was their trading symbol.

The geometric designs of this period relied heavily on a high level of brush control and, indeed, used the visible brush stokes as a part of the design, rather than employing the more common practice of simply filling in colour in an outline. As with the lustre decoration, Susie was less than happy with the durability of the thick enamel designs. The paint tended to scratch easily and flake off if applied too thickly. It is ironic that, while the geometric designs have been extremely popular in recent times and strongly identified with Susie Cooper, she herself very quickly rejected them for their impractical nature and their crude painting. The banded ware of this period is generally less attractive to collectors of the pottery, yet it is these designs of which Susie was most proud. Indeed, the most lasting influence of her work at Gray's on the pottery industry came from her development of banding as a complete decorative technique in its own right; it was now no longer just a finishing touch to a piece of pottery. Susie produced a myriad of designs, from very wide bands to thin 'string' bands, in either vibrant colour juxtapositions or mellow shades.

'Cubist' vase (*opposite above*), pattern no. 8071; Susie later came to view her designs of this period as crude.

A popular form of the twenties, this ginger jar (*opposite below*) appeared in Gray's 'Moon and Mountains' range, pattern no. 7960.

Two bold examples (*right*) of the revolutionary banded designs introduced at Gray's c. 1928.

Despite her successes, a key area of frustration for Susie was the lack of opportunity to design the ceramic shapes for her designs. She was able to produce only two: a coffee pot and a jug, produced for Gray's by Lancaster & Sandlands. In order to alleviate the frustration she felt and to pursue further her interests in fashion and textile design, Susie began to travel to London to do freelance work for the textile firm of Skelhorn & Edwards. Gray must have known that he should try to keep his star designer happy, even if it meant sharing her with another business. The largest of all Susie Cooper's works in the textile medium must surely be the main curtains she designed for the Regal Cinema chain for their Marble Arch building in late 1928. The elaborate autumnal theme of the opulent, neo-Baroque interior was given a note of restraint in her falling leaf design in gold.

At this point, Susie began to feel that her career was becoming stultified, since she could not design the pottery shapes as well as the decoration. The textile design work for Skelhorn & Edwards also came to an end in the summer of 1929. The dissatisfaction she felt at Gray's grew and, disillusioned with their range of staple designs and forms, over which she did not have total control, Susie decided she needed to leave the company. She later explained, 'Some designs would not be made because the salesmen thought they wouldn't sell. It was what they thought that provided the criteria. They would come and say, "We want something like this; this is successful." But I wanted to do what I thought. I suppose I had as much latitude in that respect as most people were allowed, perhaps more, but I still felt the confines. I wanted to do the shapes, and I wanted to do the thing all through, in my own way.'

Working at Gray's had a far-reaching and complex influence on Susie's work. The earliest experience taught her directly the discipline of piece-work, which enabled her to understand the limitations and constraints of her workers. Her later skill at utilizing the abilities of an individual to the maximum became legendary. Continued contact with Gordon Forsyth left a permanent mark on the imagery Susie employed throughout her work, especially in the shape of the scrolling forms which reappear constantly. Working at Gray's eventually frustrated Susie; she literally grew out of the situation available to her, and by 1929 she was ready to take an extraordinary step to relieve her professional frustration: to set up her own company to produce distinctive ceramics.

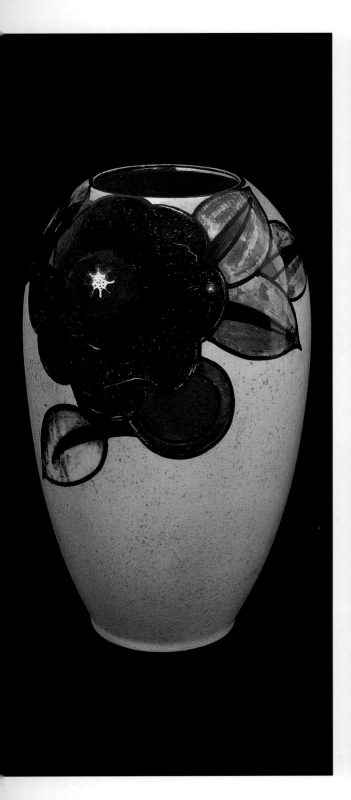

Two floral vases (*left* and *far left*) designed by Susie Cooper for Gray's; the pattern nos. are 7363 (*far left*) and 7996 (*left*).

A striped coffee set of the Gray's period (*opposite*). This is a wonderful example of Susie Cooper's dramatic sense of colour allied to form; she was also responsible for designing the pot shape.

INDEPENDENCE

1929–32

The summer of 1929 was spent by Susie Cooper in enthusiastically planning the move into business for herself. Family involvement with the scheme was very significant. And, in addition to the benefits which the long experience within the family of organizing businesses brought, Jack Beeson, Susie's brother-in-law, was prepared to break away from his horse-slaughtering company and invest the money in the development of the Susie Cooper Pottery. Jack and Hilda Beeson, his wife, hoped that their son Ted would eventually make his career with the pottery. Susie later recalled that she was often driven to succeed by the belief her family had in her and the belief she had in them.

In what was to prove one of the most remarkably difficult periods in the economic history of the twentieth century, Susie left Gray's and set up her own pottery. She later admitted: 'It was quite a bold ambition, really. Mr. Gray said, "She'll be back. Give her eight months."' Indeed, the offer of returning to work at Gray's was left open for Susie, which must have been of comfort to her and a source of hope to Gray's.

In October 1929, at the time of the Wall Street Crash, Susie installed herself in part of a building known as the George Street Pottery in Tunstall; she had just two rooms, a large paint shop and a small office. Jack Beeson took on the role of sales director and was the most substantial investor. Albert G. Richardson, or 'A.G.', as he was known, a well-established and respected potter, came from Crown Ducal, after an introduction by Gordon Forsyth, to ensure the quality of the wares at the George Street Pottery. It was a shrewd move on his part to make the link with the noted young designer who had revolutionized the output of Gray's. Just six paintresses were employed. Alice Hancock had moved with Susie from Gray's and was from then on to be Susie's right-hand assistant.

The other girls (Nora Dickinson, Mary Taylor, Cissie Hand, Louie Pickin and Clara Bolton) were all set to work initially on refurbishing the workshop and offices of George Street. Susie immediately wanted to give an 'artistic look' to the business and accordingly the walls were whitewashed and the paintresses' stools painted in bright colours. Susie later reminisced about the first day's work, especially the sight of Nora Dickinson rising from her stool and wincing over its hardness. The atmosphere, however, was one of diligence and camaraderie. The designs of the fledgeling business show an immediate shift from the type of work she had produced for Gray's, though a jug painted at George Street illustrates the relatively poor quality of the wares produced there. Susie later remembered being horrified by the lumpy, pitted wares, which she attempted to improve with bold, all-over patterns. These pieces were marked with a thin rubber stamped mark bearing the words

An early under-glaze design (no. A60); Susie Cooper later recalled that she found the quality of the George Street pottery 'shocking', feeling obliged to use all-over designs to cover flaws in the body. This design was re-entered in the pattern books later as E170.

Pattern no. E184 (*above*); this 'Console' vase is the only known
example of this shape and pattern, characterized by its stark
'cog-wheel' forms.

This colourful selection of jugs (*opposite*) is drawn from the early years of
independent production; from top, left to right: 'Lotus' shape with pattern
E111, 'Stepped' shape 'Campanulas' E308, 'Paris' shape 'Briar Rose' E328,
'Ross' shape E215, 'Melbourne' shape E66, 'Venice' shape E485, 'Dutch'
shape 'Citrons' E194, 'Melbourne' shape 'Tulips' E61 and 'Dutch' shape E309.

A ginger jar, c. 1930 (*below*); Susie once recalled, 'The poor deer were always
being chased across my pottery.'

'A Susie Cooper Production' within a triangle; this may well
have been derived from her own personal rebus mark at Gray's.

Susie never doubted that her business would eventually succeed. She knew that there was room for something different and
she certainly needed all her conviction when she was forced to leave
the new premises after only three weeks. The owners of the George
Street site had been in financial difficulty and their creditors fore-
closed on them. Susie later recalled that there had been just one
firing of her works at George Street. Obviously, the pieces bearing
the triangular Tunstall mark which survive are extremely rare.

A rather grim winter then passed, as Susie and Jack Beeson
looked for other suitable premises for the new business. Finally,
in March of 1930 Susie and her team moved into the Chelsea
Works, a small pottery site owned by Doulton's. This factory was
located on Moorland Road in Burslem, barely a stone's throw
from the Burslem School of Art. An initial rental was agreed
and it was planned that Doulton's should supply the white
ware for decoration. 'A.G.' helped with some initial preparation
of the kiln, but was then only slightly involved in the business,
eventually leaving the Potteries to teach at the Royal College of Art
in London. Susie remembered the kiln at the Chelsea Works with
fondness, because it 'fired beautifully'. The firing was apparently
slow which, she felt, produced good strong colours. In charge of
the kiln was Jack Shufflebotham, who had come to work for Susie
from the liquidated George Street Pottery.

Due to the delays caused by the failure of George Street, Susie
decided to get the paintresses working as quickly as possible, and
so she shelved her plans for producing the actual wares. Instead,
she scoured the Potteries for the best and cheapest white ware,
finding that the Depression had made many manufacturers eager
for business – so Susie was able to buy the white blanks at very
competitive prices. Her suppliers at this time were Grimwades Ltd.,
Grindley & Co. Ltd., Doulton & Co., and Wood & Sons; the
manufacturers' names were painted over with black enamel.

Patterns were entered in a thick foolscap ledger called the
Description Book. It appears that the Susie Cooper Pottery, like
many new businesses, attempted to conceal its newness by beginning the pattern numbers at E50, the letter 'E' denoting earthenware. Susie displayed a great deal of business acumen in the design
of her first patterns, which were a highly saleable balance of floral,
banded and modernistic designs. The overall impression of the
designs that survive from this early period is one of great freshness,
with an emphasis upon a whiter body rather than a yellow glaze.
The few patterns which were produced at George Street were either
entered in the Description Book or given 'A' numbers 50–61, noted
down much later.

The 'modernist' designs, as Susie most often labelled them, are
quite astonishing in their stark abstraction. The design E69, with
the appearance of a multi-coloured circuit board, resembles a painting by Mondrian, and shows Susie's undoubted awareness of
International Modernism. Even such a mundane object as a cheese
wedge was given the 'modernist' treatment by Susie; E88, using an
economical three-colour scheme, is surely as daring an abstract
design as has ever been applied to table-ware. Such designs raised
quite a few eyebrows when they were first displayed.

The firm placed its first advertisement in the *The Pottery Gazette*
in April 1930. Susie's idea of the image of the business she wished
to create was very evident in this early piece of publicity. The wide
margins and simplicity of the layout denote the special quality of
Susie Cooper design, while the wording, 'Elegance combined with
utility', was to prove an apt description of her approach throughout
her life. Even the leaping deer displayed in the advertisement was

destined to make a dramatic appearance a little later on. The article on the Susie Cooper Pottery in the same issue of the journal seems to have been written in a spirit of surprise and confusion: 'There is something that savours of the unique in connection with the formation of this new company, in as much as it is only rarely, in the history of the Staffordshire Potteries, that one comes across an instance of a pottery artist – and particularly a lady – who has the confidence and courage to attempt to carve out a career by laying down a special plant and staff on what must be admitted to be something suggestive of a commercial scale.' The notion of a woman in the industry in Susie's position was truly unique at that time. But it was also her temerity in setting up – within a very brief period of time – a new business during tremendously depressed times for the pottery industry, coupled with her extraordinary designs, which created the buzz of adventure around the enterprise.

In response to the feature in *The Pottery Gazette*, the Nottingham store of Griffin & Spalding sent their buyer, a Miss Langford, to see Susie at the pottery. This resulted in an order for a range of wares, and so the Susie Cooper Pottery was at last up and running.

The designs entered in the Description Book are indicative of the sophisticated range of styles produced by the young business. 'The Pasture', a nursery-ware design, incorporated a collection of farmyard animals, including a piglet, donkey, cow and lamb, with a 'wee maid' in a blue dress to watch over them. The evocatively titled 'The Storm', in tango orange, black, grey and yellow, conjured up the tumultuous colouring of a storm. Examples of a series of mottled colour-effect vases produced at the same time have, tantalizingly, remained untraced to the present day. Sketchy pencil illustrations and brief descriptions give us their swirling and wavy lines in brown, grey, black and yellow. Perhaps they should be seen as the forerunners of the painted studio wares. Susie's visual language, even at this early stage, is almost complete. Her menagerie of animal subjects was growing rapidly, while the leaping deer, freed from the rigidity of the Deco painting of its Gray's incarnation, makes many dynamic and stylized dashes across her pottery and advertising designs.

J.J. Adams, known as Jack Adams within the trade, was chosen as the London agent of Cooper pottery. The Adams showroom was at 13 Charterhouse Street, Holborn, a property leased from another company for which Adams was also agent, and a small fee was charged for the space occupied by the Susie Cooper wares. Adams later recalled that these were extremely successful from the beginning. On his rounds of the major stores, such as Harrod's, Selfridge's and Thos. Goode, the china departments clamoured for the

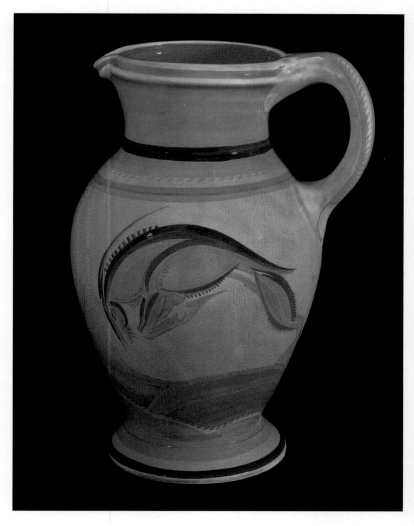

This remarkably elegant jug (*above*), dated 6 July 1931, was part of a series of designs which featured various animal forms painted freehand.

Susie Cooper patterns and Adams found he could not get enough to meet demand. Despite taking on more paintresses, Susie Cooper Productions obviously needed new premises.

During this period it had emerged that the pottery blanks supplied by Wood & Sons offered the best value for Susie; they were reasonably priced and of good quality. It was therefore decided that a move to premises adjoining Wood's, across Burslem, would be particularly advantageous. Will Lloyd, the works manager at Wood's, arranged with Jack Beeson for Harry Wood to visit the Chelsea Works to form an impression of the quality of the work. He must have been suitably impressed, since Susie took time during the traditional Potteries' holiday to visit the Wood's factory at the Crown Works, to which she finally moved in August 1931; this was to be the scene of her greatest triumphs for nearly fifty years.

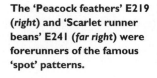

The 'Cube' shape (*opposite*), here as a breakfast set in pattern no. E298, was sold in limited quantities between 1931 and 1934.

The 'Peacock feathers' E219 (*right*) and 'Scarlet runner beans' E241 (*far right*) were forerunners of the famous 'spot' patterns.

CHAPTER FOUR

This breakfast set (*opposite*), pattern E284, made in 1932, includes an early 'Kestrel' tea pot. As the 'Kestrel' range was expanded to include more shapes, Susie was able to move forward from such eclectic collections as this.

THE LEAPING DEER

1932–34

The stepped jug form, used for a short time in the early nineteen-thirties, was not in fact a Susie Cooper design. This example is decorated with pattern E314, which fits neatly on to the bands of the body.

The first few years of the nineteen-thirties can reasonably be thought of as the most dynamic and fertile in the working life of Susie Cooper. A dazzling succession of experiments and innovations caused a sensation within the industry. Seemingly everything she set her hand to was a triumph; the business expanded rapidly and began to export a substantial part of the production to foreign markets.

The new site of the pottery, the Crown Works on Newcastle Street, was a wing of Wood & Sons' subsidiary, Bursley. It had previously been used by Charlotte and Frederick Rhead, and now provided Susie and her twenty or so staff with ample space. The owner of the factory, Harry Wood, struck up a close working relationship with her, which augured well for both parties. Wood was not only letting the building in the severe economic conditions, he was letting it to a rising star in pottery design. In return, Susie was to be supplied with a steady supply of good-quality, inexpensive wares and, crucially, to have the opportunity of producing her own shapes. Her complete control over production was to yield dramatic results.

The move to the Crown Works promised a great deal, and Susie now reeled off a dazzling array of diverse designs, from the most subtle floral to stripped, uncompromising abstraction. One of the most lyrical of these abstract designs is 'Galaxy' E282. Susie recalled that this was one of the first done at the Crown Works. These early designs seem to have been given the triangular rubber

The 'Galaxy' pattern E282 on 'Cube' tea-ware was one of the first designs produced at the Crown Works, a deliberate departure from the heavy geometric designs of Gray's.

The 'Kestrel' range was one of the longest lived of all Susie Cooper designs; this collection of coffee pots (*opposite*) covers the years 1932–50, with pattern nos. (*from top, left to right*) 824, 478, 912, 2043, 1341, 474, 2206, 776, 898, 1252, 2200, 1342, 1337, 1894, 1574 and 2068.

Susie Cooper streamlined the Wood's tankard shape (*right*), applying a range of banded designs, E418 (*right*) and E410 (*far right*).

Table-ware (*far right*) in pattern no. E279, with unusual broken banding and geometric shapes.

stamp mark, though Susie soon felt that the fresh start at the Crown Works should be celebrated with a new back stamp. The leaping deer now sprang into view yet again, this time in a highly prominent way as a detailed lithograph back stamp. The form of the deer seemed the perfect representation of Susie Cooper design – dynamism with poise and grace. From this point onwards Susie exercised full control over the image she wished to promote and the business she wanted to build.

A tankard used by Wood's as a promotional item for breweries was soon reworked by Susie. Its handle was given a new, streamlined form, while the ribbing of the main body was used as a guide for supremely economical banding and more striking motifs. The importance Susie attached to the unity of shape and decoration is clear in the multitude of designs produced for the tankards; at the same time she continued the mixture of floral and more avant-garde designs in other wares, which ensured sales over the widest possible range of tastes.

Work systems were established at the factory very quickly. These followed six-monthly cycles, with the build-up for the Christmas trade being a peak, followed by preparation for the trade shows in March. Alice Hancock, Susie's 'right hand' from the time at Gray's, would quite often work with her employer on a design and provide the finishes, such as bands and borders. The pair would frequently stay late at the factory to meet deadlines on samples and commissions. Alice was very slow with free-hand painting, but also exceptionally good, so Susie removed her from piece-work, since the money she earned did not reflect her ability. Alice also played a major role in the training of paintresses, where her fastidiousness was influential in the creation of a highly skilled work-force. Both women were quiet during work and would sit in the decorating area, known as the paint shop, creating designs, trying out new methods and perfecting decoration techniques. Though it is quite accurate to say that all the designs were by Susie Cooper, the development of the free-hand painting was a shared responsibility with Alice Hancock and another paintress, Nora Dickinson, who had joined the team just before the move to the Chelsea Works.

Susie Cooper's trade stand at the 1932 British Industries Fair carried her first major shape design. The 'Kestrel' shape embodied all of Susie's ideas about design: things should be both stylish and useful. The coffee and tea pots of the range have a distinctly sculptural feel to them; there is balance of movement on a vertical axis, as the handle tapers downwards and the spout rears up. The bulbous bodies provide a solid foundation for the drama of the shapes

attached to them, and the kestrel crest crowns the design with a streamlined flourish. Above all, the new table-wares worked brilliantly. The spouts of the coffee and tea pots are so finely poised and potted that they pour perfectly. The covers have a lock flange which prevents them from falling off during pouring. The success of this design feature has meant that remarkably few 'Kestrel' pots have survived without damage to the excellent lock after years of impatient, unknowing rattling to remove the covers.

The Pottery Gazette reported of the stand at the exhibition: 'The Susie Cooper Pottery ... exhibited a very smart and distinctive array of pieces in hand-painted pottery, truly individualistic in its character. This was displayed upon a stand which was itself totally unlike anything else in the fair; everyone could see that it had been evolved by Miss Susie Cooper herself, an artist of the modern school of thought – imaginative and at times a trifle audacious.... There was constantly a crowd of admirers around the stand, and the Queen herself was arrested by what she saw here, and, entering the stand, conversed with Miss Cooper and made purchases.' Queen Mary bought a 'Briar Rose' E328 breakfast-in-bed set, and the Princess Royal, another member of the party, a 'Clown' lamp base.

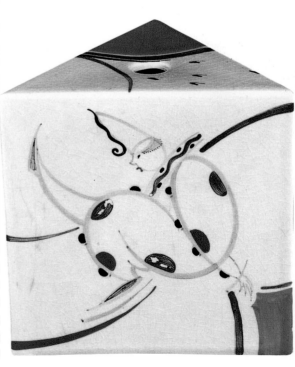

The 'Clown' lamp base E354; it was this piece which particularly caught the eye of members of the Royal Family on a visit to the British Industries Fair in 1932. Only a handful of examples are known to exist.

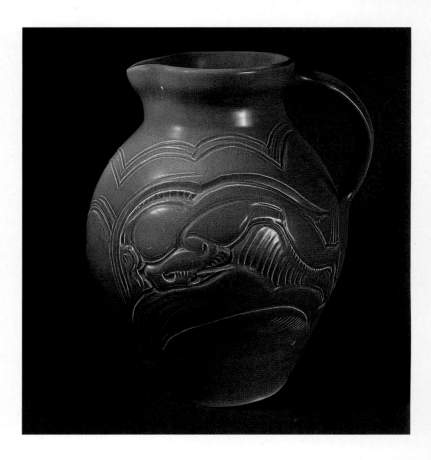

Two examples of hand-carved 'studio' jugs of the early nineteen-thirties (*above left and right*): the 'Kestrel' jug in the 'Acorn' E324 pattern (*left*) was the first such; 'Rams' E325 (*right*) dates from 1932. Many later examples of carved ware were slip-cast moulded versions.

A bowl (*left*), decorated with the 'Stylized leaves' 685 pattern; foliage became a key motif at Susie Cooper Productions. This example was produced using the under-glaze technique which Susie sought to add to her range of decorative techniques at this period.

The ability to produce under-glaze decoration had always been one of Susie's key ambitions and now, in a triumphant mood, she had Wood's potters throw a range of vases and other decorative wares to her specifications. These shapes she used as the basis for a range of carved and painted 'studio' wares. The first of these carved designs was 'Acorn' E324 and soon there followed a vast range of other stylized plant forms and animal subjects. The designs were pounced, which involved pricking holes in the shape of the design in tissue paper and then dusting through the holes on to the pot with charcoal. Once the guide-marks were in place, the unfired clay was carved with a sharp tool. As the demand for the studio pots grew, the range was slip-cast, with the design sharpened by hand. Over the years a string of abstract lines and motifs joined the natural subjects.

The painted studio pots, which emerged probably at the same time as the carved pieces, were very much a favourite of Susie's. She found the way that the colours of the designs changed when the cream body glaze was applied an unexpected delight. A keen experimenter, she carefully noted the colours, then composed them. A trade review of the pottery at the time remarked that the painted studio pots were produced with the vogue for mottled tile mantle-pieces in mind. Clearly, the colouring of the pottery was an important consideration in finding ways to complement this aspect of interior decoration. The fact that this matching was taken so seriously points again to the astute marketing and overall design concerns of the Cooper Pottery.

'Graduated black bands' (*above*) was an enormously successful design which ran from c. 1933 to 1940 and was exported in large quantities. The coffee pot and cup are from the 'Kestrel' range; the pattern no. of the large plate is 784.

Painted 'studio' wares, c. 1932–33 (*opposite below right* and *left*); such works as the jug were often trial pieces which Susie particularly relished decorating; the beaker has the 'Orchids' M72 pattern.

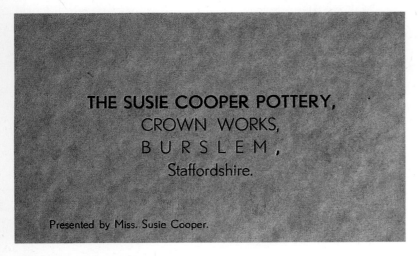

Susie Cooper's business card (*above left*) of the period.

Banding as a complete design had by this stage been taken up by many manufacturers as staple decoration. The constant desire for refinement and experiment, however, led Susie to wash-banding, a development which kept her ahead of her competitors. She found that the enamel colours, when diluted with turpentine in certain quantities, produced highly subtle gradations of tone when banded. The range of patterns produced by this method was an instant success; the myriad of colour schemes were sophisticated in appearance and yet relatively inexpensive to produce. Again, a strong feeling for the market is evident in the new designs, which became known as 'Wedding Ring'; they were to be a staple source of income for the pottery for over thirty years. Their popularity was reported in the *The Pottery Gazette* in 1934: 'A pattern was brought out some little time ago by Miss Susie Cooper, the Newcastle Street Pottery at Burslem — a remarkable and distinctive decoration embodying the use of an unusual red. It was a pattern well received in the States. And with what result? To quote from a letter which recently came to hand: "No fewer than four different American factories have copied this line, and one of them has even had the nerve to call their version of it 'Susan's Red'."' The skill of the Susie

Cooper paintresses, however, meant that the copies looked like a pale imitation of the originals and the major outlets remained loyal to the real thing.

Official recognition of Susie's outstanding work was marked with her appointment to the newly created Society of Industrial Artists. In this capacity, she took part in numerous debates and lectures, further highlighting her remarkable position as a woman in a male-dominated industry. Although notoriously quietly spoken, Susie repeatedly asserted her ideas and values at the meetings with great confidence and conviction. The most famous of those debates was probably the one in Stoke-on-Trent in which Serge Chermayeff, the modernist architect and designer, decried the excesses of over-decorated goods, calling for simple, undecorated wares from the pottery industry. Susie Cooper quietly but firmly replied by asking what would become of all those reliant upon the decoration of pottery for their livelihoods. The evening with Chermayeff also remained memorable for Susie for a personal reason; it was after the lecture that she met her future husband, the architect Cecil Barker.

A buyer for the department store of John Lewis paid the Susie Cooper Pottery a visit on the day before the British Industries Fair in February 1933. Susie later recalled having to unpack pieces to show the buyer, a Mrs. McDermot. Clearly impressed with what she saw, the latter ordered two banded patterns, E475 and E481, for open stock, meaning that the pottery would be available for purchase as individual pieces as well as in sets. The order was extremely lucrative for Susie and was the beginning of a long and fruitful relationship with John Lewis.

Examples of 'Susan's Red' E479 (*opposite*), one of her most imitated wash-banding patterns; wares produced with these design techniques were especially popular with large stores who clamoured for exclusive designs, requests which sometimes had to be satisfied by simple reversal as in pattern no. 1112 seen here on the large platter.

Susie Cooper wares (*below*) displayed in a thirties modernist setting in the Woburn Place showroom of her London agent in 1934.

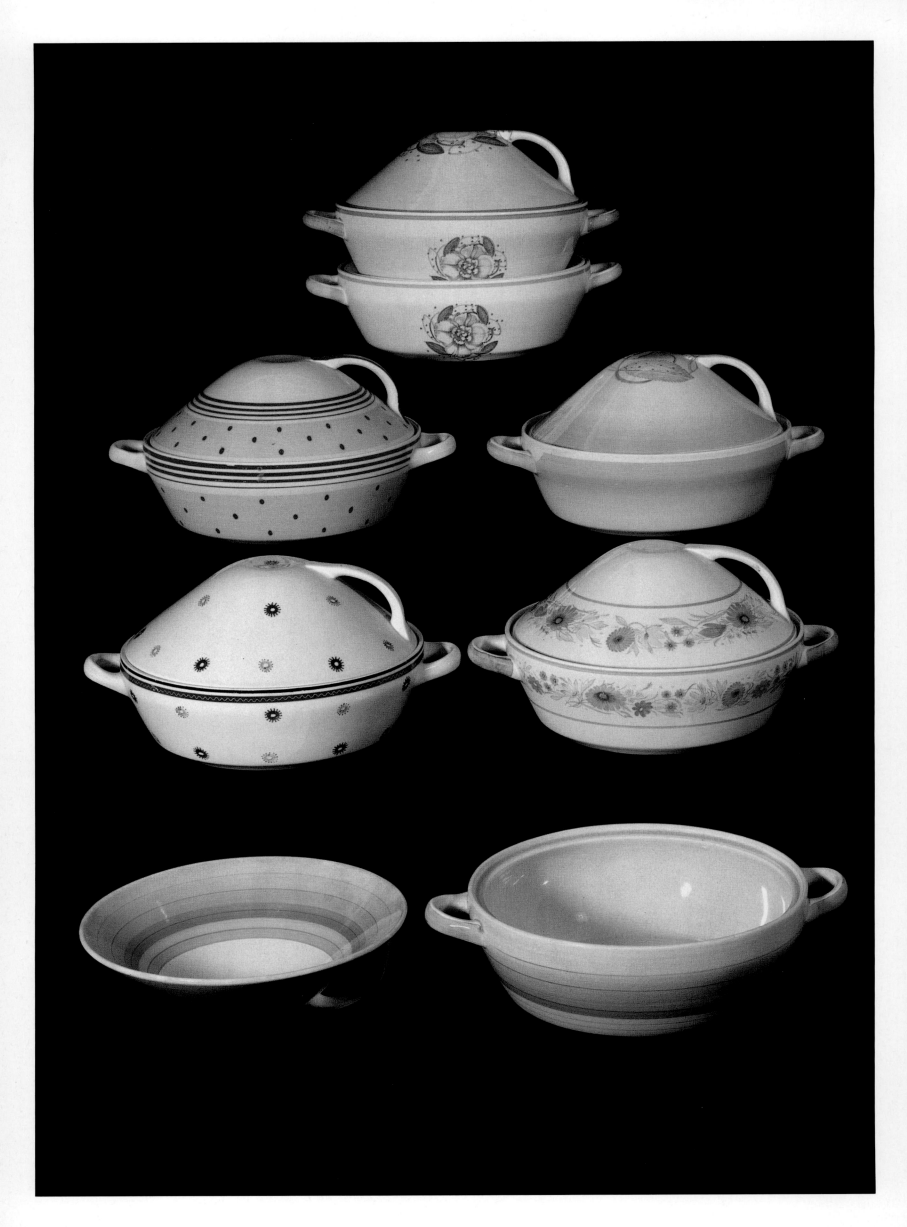

These 'Kestrel' tureens (*opposite*)date from c. 1933 to 1952 in pattern nos. (*from top, left to right*) 2281, 1342, 1160, 2068, 2286 and 695. The cover doubled as a second dish, while the full body lent itself easily to many types of decoration.

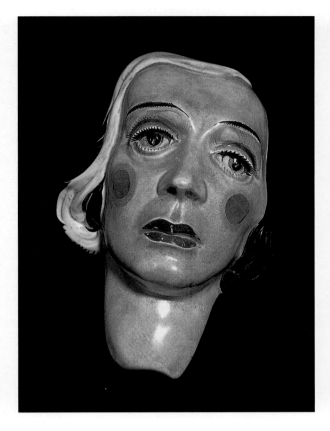 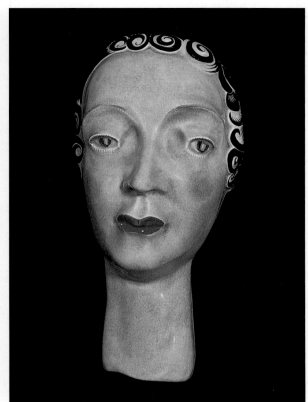

Only small numbers of the wall masks of 1933 (*right*) were produced; the portrait of Greta Garbo (*right*) was sold as 'Brunette', and Susie Cooper's self-portrait (*far right*) as 'Blonde'.

The British Industries Fair of 1933 was of especial significance for the Susie Cooper Pottery; not only did it see the introduction of the studio ranges, but also the appearance of the 'Kestrel' cover dish. Indeed, so enthusiastic was the reception for this tureen that Susie soon had a patent applied to the product. The lid of the cover dish doubled as a dish in its own right when turned upside down; the handle, placed stylishly to one side, provided the support. Not only did the dishes stack for space-saving convenience, but steam from any hot foods inside dripped back into the tureen. With the 'Kestrel' range now complete, Susie Cooper design could be seen to be at the heart of modernist functionalism.

To cap the successes of the first half of 1933, the Pottery was asked to take part in the Dorland Hall Exhibition during the summer. This exhibition was intended by its organizers, the Design and Industries Association, to raise the profile of modern design. Susie showed a range of pottery, the most notable being her new 'Curlew' wares, with bold calligraphic designs. Its dramatic streamlined form was something of an exercise in style by Susie. But the shape, while supremely stylish, was less flexible when it came to the application of patterns and was therefore quite limited in use and production.

In an article in the *Manchester Evening News* in March 1933, Susie highlighted one of the key reasons for her success: namely, the education of her employees and the best use of their abilities. Some of 'my girls' had come to her straight from school, others from the local art school; Susie took her responsibilities for training them and keeping them in employment very seriously indeed. Some attended art school for part of the day and then worked in the factory for the rest. She regarded the factory as being rather like a school, 'only more so!' Every day they were supposed to learn something more until their training was complete. 'They are such nice girls', she wrote, 'eager and teachable and happy; their painting seems to develop all the best in them. They take such a pride in it. They have to be delicate and skilful, and generally they are gentle and refined, too. They soon acquire all the pride of a true craftsman.'

Susie Cooper was now part of the design élite in the United Kingdom and widely respected. The export markets also began to be developed in earnest, considerable amounts of table-ware now being supplied to major stores in the United States and Canada.

This 'Curlew' tea pot (*above*) is decorated with pattern no. 616.

A promotional photograph of 1933 (*below*) shows the growing range of 'studio' wares produced by the pottery.

EXPANSION AND DISASTER

1 9 3 4 – 4 5

At the end of 1933, *The Pottery Gazette* reported on further remarkable progress at the Susie Cooper Pottery, especially in the design of shapes and in ornamentation. Experimentation had continued unabated there, with the introduction of Susie's crayon designs. Believing that the lumps of colour used to mark firing trials could be put to a more creative use, she had sticks of the colour made up for her; used on biscuit pottery these crayons produced very distinctive textured lines. The first crayon design entered in the pattern book is 'Pink hydrangea' 657, a delicate, simplified floral motif, highlighted with black under-glaze paint.

It was not long before Susie saw the real potential of the crayon technique, as she designed clutches of abstract motifs and leaf forms. Simple crayon lines with or without accompanying painted lines began to characterize the pottery's output. In spite of Susie's, and the public's, liking for this technique, it was not popular with all the paintresses, as the sensation of applying crayon to biscuit pottery can be likened to that of fingernails scraping on a blackboard. Nevertheless, the pieces produced in this way were extremely successful and, crucially at that time of rapid expansion of the business, this type of decoration could be applied very quickly.

As markets expanded, so too the pottery had to step up production to meet demands, and printed decoration seemed a natural way forward. Susie had for several years used printed outlines with the addition of hand-painted enamel; 'Freesia', 'Shepherd's purse fritillary' and early versions of 'Nosegay' utilized this technique. Lithograph printing was brought into the production with design 930, now known as 'Two leaf spray'. The visual dexterity of Susie and her unique style are clearly visible in the collection of lithograph designs she produced over the next few years – designs of such subtlety that they seem to have the quality of hand painting; it was this quality which surprised and thrilled the industry.

This selection of crayon designs includes the first design in the technique, 'Pink hydrangea' 657, produced as a trial plate in 1933, with five-colour scrolling and leaves; the breakfast hot-water jug was made for Susie Cooper's own use at the time of her wedding in 1938 and bears the initials 'S.V.B.' – Susie Vera Barker.

This group of pieces decorated in crayon banding demonstrates the subtle effects obtainable by the technique.

Not everything went smoothly from the outset, however; Susie's initial relationship with the printers of the lithographs was fraught with problems.

It was a time-honoured tradition for designs to be submitted to the printers by the pottery manufacturer and then for the draughtsmen and draughtswomen at the print shop to produce the colour separations for the printing process. Susie began to have grave doubts about this way of working when 'Two leaf spray' was produced in a green colour variation. To her horror, she found that the form of the motif had been changed. Furious, she contacted the printers, told them that she could see that someone else had done the green version, and that this was reason enough for her to do the preparatory work herself. Eventually she won this battle over established working practices. One drawback of the lithographic process, however, was the increased cost of the wares. The lithograph designs were more likely to produce seconds or rejects than hand painting and so were slightly more expensive to produce.

In 1935 Harry Wood approached Susie Cooper to design a floral lithograph for his own productions. She eventually came up with a floral spray which was traditional yet also carried the mark of her unique approach to design. This was 'Dresden Spray'; Wood, however, did not think it would be possible to produce the lithograph, as it was too complex and unusual. Its designer later recalled: 'The second I had finished the "Dresden" and fitted it up for the borders … Harry Wood said, "I don't know whether I dare". I said, "Well, if you're not going to do it, I'll do it myself."' And Susie paid for the experiment herself although, with a minimum order of 2000 sheets at the lithograph printers, a failure would have been very costly indeed. But just as Susie had believed, the success of 'Dresden Spray' was absolute; the industry was amazed at its technical and artistic virtuosity and the public loved it. A sign of the popularity of the design is that 'Dresden Spray' continued until earthenware production was stopped nearly thirty years later. The design, however, has remained a great favourite with collectors, especially in the Far East.

In the same year Susie Cooper produced a spot pattern, called 'Polka Dot'. This was developed as a design which a new paintress could produce while in training. Training typically took two years and so use of the trainees in the decorating of wares was a crucial economic and production factor in the business. The patterns, in at least four colour variations (tangerine, apple green, blue and yellow), were taken by the John Lewis and Peter Jones department stores as open stock in various combinations. 'Polka Dot' has perhaps come

Two prints by Susie Cooper; 'Dresden Spray' (*top*) may be regarded as conservative by the standard of her other designs, but it did in fact pose an enormous challenge in the context of lithographic printing; 'Patricia Rose' (*above*) received many different treatments over four decades.

These hand-painted wares (*left*), decorated with animal forms, were unfortunately destroyed during World War II.

Plates from the late thirties: 'Deer' (*top*) and 'Tiger' (*above*), pattern no. S974.

to epitomize the salient qualities of Susie Cooper design: it is supremely economic in both visual qualities and in execution; it also has complete unity of decoration and form.

The working practices of the Susie Cooper Pottery were by now well known and respected within the industry. The building was kept in immaculate condition, with cleanliness being of paramount importance. This was because decoration would be adversely affected by impurities in the materials or on the pottery. Once, when Susie was visiting the Wood's production area, she found it to be untidy and the floors grimy. She quietly but firmly had the room cleared and the floors washed down, only allowing the workers to continue when it met with her approval. The painting shops were disciplined areas, with talking between the girls kept to a minimum, while Susie quite often sat at the end of the room, working on designs with Alice. She was known as a demanding employer and the girls in the workshop were fully aware that they were not expected to 'step out of line'. In later years it became something of a gentle tease to call Susie a slave-driver. She would typically reply, 'I've got a reputation for being a slave-driver, I believe I have. It's not true, really. It's just pure enthusiasm.'

In the middle of this period of increasing acclaim and business expansion, Susie still found time to execute a uniquely personal work, a figure she called 'Lummox'. This figure of a woman with head bowed was made by Susie in the first half of 1935 after reading a book by the American author Fanny Hurst. The central character of the book was described by Susie as being 'a woman who was put upon, taken advantage of'. The suffering of the character is

The very personal figure of 'Lummox'; sculpted by Susie Cooper in 1935, she still regarded it as one of her finest works sixty years later.

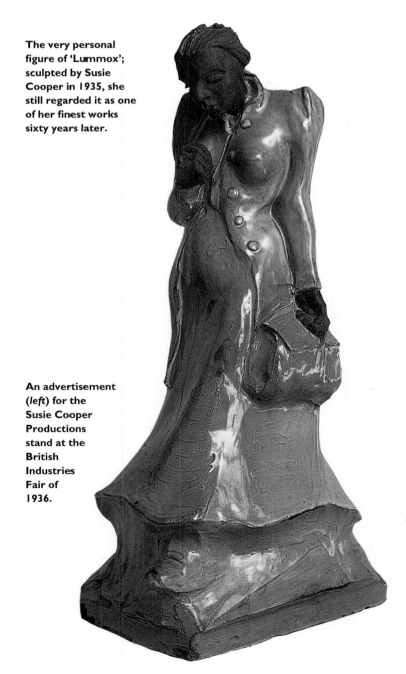

An advertisement (*left*) for the Susie Cooper Productions stand at the British Industries Fair of 1936.

In the layout of her stands at the British Industries Fairs, Susie preferred a modernist, uncluttered look (*above* and *right*). The exterior of her stand at the 1938 fair (*top right*), especially, shows the influence of International Modernism on her approach to design.

indeed clear in the artist's portrayal: the expressiveness of the torso, especially, shows an understanding of womanhood far more complex than that seen, for example, in the fetishistic figurines so popular in the nineteen-twenties and -thirties. The solid body of the figure shows the artist uniting materials and form to create a work of great strength. Susie later described the figure, 'The "Lummox" you see is a big, bulky, awkward sort of creature. I could see such a strong mental picture of her. I felt I would like to put it down and the red clay seemed the proper medium for it. It is quite a weight, but that is part of the character of the thing. You can't imagine that being in china.'

Nursery wares again became prominent in the displays of the Susie Cooper Pottery, especially in 1936 and 1938. Sailing boats, trains, marching toy soldiers and a jack-in-the-box joined a menagerie of exotic and farmyard animals lithographed across the surface of a whole range of pottery.

In March 1938 *The Pottery and Glass Record* summarized the trade's increasingly deferential approach to Susie Cooper Pottery productions when it described a set in the 'Fern' 1534 design, at the British Industries Fair, as 'characteristically Cooperesque'. And Susie did have a strikingly inventive approach to set composition. The profit margin on cups and saucers had always been low, so Susie decided that sets for special use, such as salad, fruit, soup, game, buffet and *hors d'oeuvres*, were necessary for financial viability. For some of the wares, particularly those intended for *hors d'oeuvres*, limed oak trays were designed and sold with the ceramics, making the sets ideal gifts. The creation of smaller sets and a flexibility in set composition were seen very much as moving with the times and

changing life-styles. Purchasers could add to their sets over a period of time, gradually amassing the variety of wares to suit their needs. Susie certainly knew her market, designing for 'professional people, younger people, people with taste but not much money'.

A string of commissions underlined the wide appeal and acceptance of Susie Cooper Pottery production in the latter half of the nineteen-thirties. Imperial Airways commissioned services for their international routes; the three designs produced combined either painted decoration of the Imperial Airways monogram or aerographed and sgraffito decoration. Three designs were produced with a portcullis motif in pinks and fawn for use in the House of Lords restaurant at the Palace of Westminster. The relationship with International Modernism was maintained by the use of Susie Cooper pottery in the restaurants of the experimental Peckham

The business of Susie Cooper Productions was substantially expanded during the late thirties by the introduction of special sets, such as this buffet and salad set (*below*) in the 'Scrolls and stars' pattern 1828.

Conscious of the importance of the North American markets, a series of special wares were introduced with appropriate themes, such as this 'Thanksgiving Turkey' platter (*above*).

Other special lines of this period included nursery-ware decorated with both hand-painted and lithographed animals (*below*) which could be ordered personalized with a particular child's name. 'Noah's Ark' (*right*) provided another opportunity for the use of animal motifs.

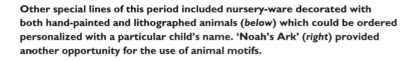

The beginning of the war years: these service plates (*above*) with fruit subjects date from c. 1940.

In spite of the ominous signs for the immediate future, the late thirties had many high points for Susie Cooper, not the least her marriage to Cecil Barker (the wedding party seen below in the grounds of what was to be the couple's home, the Old Parsonage at Dilhorn), for which a special service with dark green sgraffito decoration was made (*right*).

Health Centre, opened in 1935, and of the Peter Jones department store, opened in 1936 – both buildings were celebrated examples of modernist architecture.

On 28 April 1938, Susie Cooper was married to Cecil Barker. The wedding reception was held at the Old Parsonage at Dilhorn, which was to be the family home. People who knew Susie well were surprised that she should get married; it had seemed to many that she was far too busy making a success of her business. The contrast between Susie's modernist principles and Cecil's classical architectural training is sometimes said to have been a source of tension.

While it is true that Cecil raised an eyebrow from time to time at some of the more abstract and stylized designs of his wife, his own education had, in many ways, a close affinity with International Modernism, to which bear witness the many successful projects they undertook jointly over many years.

Joy Couper, who later became a close friend of Susie, began work at the pottery as a paintress in 1938. Susie's attention was particularly drawn to Joy because of her family connections with the pottery industry; John Butler, her father, who had died in 1936, had been the highly respected art director at Wood & Sons and done much to develop glazes at firms such as Wilkinson's. Susie soon noticed his daughter's considerable abilities and the two women became firm friends. Joy was eventually seconded from the paint shop to help Susie find a use for wasted biscuit-ware stock which was kept stacked in an outbuilding. It was decided that a range of freehand designs should be applied to the wares, and Joy set about decorating them with such motifs as stylized leaf patterns. These were then passed to Susie, who would embellish them subtly, giving them the unmistakable flourish of a Cooper production. The under-glaze designs produced in this way were for export, and the most beautiful of the freehand scrolling leaves and other stylized foliage

Susie Cooper was a woman of striking looks, well documented in these portraits of 1938, including perhaps the best-known of all her photographs – that of the artist with the 'Lummox' figure (*right*). Another series of startling portraits (*below left* and *right*) came about after a request by Eatons of Canada for publicity shots. These were taken in the London studio of Cleo Cottrell and, although taken by a studio assistant, capture sensitively a whole range of moods and poses, from the robust and business-like to the self-consciously enigmatic and glamorous.

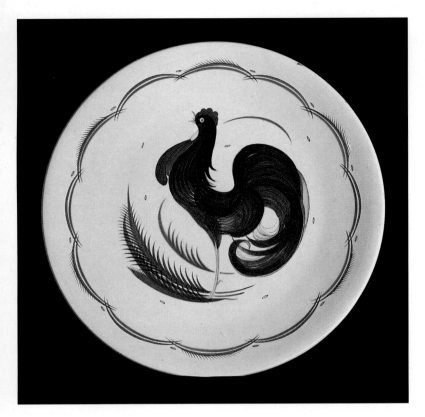

This 'Rooster' plate, dating from the late nineteen-thirties, was another specific response to the United States market.

designs seem now to turn up most frequently in the United States and Canada. It is probable that many of these oddities were not entered in the pattern books and so now provide yet another area of mystery for collectors. Patterns such as those partly designed by Joy Couper sometimes reappeared later as a lithograph border; one such is 'Beechwood' 1790.

The huge demand for Susie Cooper wares in North America led to increased tailoring of the factory output for this market. Although Susie had no direct knowledge of her export markets, she contrived to produce a range of specialist goods to satisfy her over-

seas customers, including a number of glamorous items for social occasions, such as cocktail trays and huge punch bowls with matching cups and coasters. The 'Thanksgiving Turkey' sets produced in copious quantities for the United States market were for a rather more traditional family gathering. The firm of Fondeville and Co. in New York was so successful with its Susie Cooper sales that it acquired the United States patent for wash-banding designs, and on a number of occasions actively pursued copyright infringement on Susie Cooper's and on its own behalf. It was Gene Fondeville who inspired the range of table centres which appeared in the latter half of the nineteen-thirties. The leaping deer table centre, now an icon of Susie Cooper pottery, together with a fox and hound and flower troughs as surround date from this period. The table centre figures were designed in three colourways to match the enormously successful 'Wedding Ring' services. The publicity material of Fondeville and Co. ended on a bold note: 'Come in and see our new patterns in Susie Cooper Ware – the favourite contemporary designer of smart brides and hostesses of three continents.'

The ambitions and energy of Susie at this time seem to have been limitless. The number of items passing through the kiln in a week had reached the very respectable total of two thousand dozen by 1939–40. This figure includes larger pieces which were counted as two or three items. With her business thus assured, Susie managed to find time to work on yet another project.

In the spring of 1939 she began to plan the production of children's clothing and by the early summer she had produced a detailed portfolio of some twenty or so designs. Susie Cooper Miniatures was to be the name of the venture, with the clothing being made by her sister Agnes's dress-making business. The portfolio was so lively and exquisitely drawn that Susie secured the interest and support of Harrod's. It seemed that she was about to conquer new territory. But when the business was almost ready for launching and even a brass plaque bearing the company name made for the exterior of the Crown Works, war broke out and

Yet another quirkily conceived American line: these 'Moustache' cups were very much an oddity in the whole Susie Cooper range, but perhaps pattern no. 1326 did conform to the values of 'elegance with utility'.

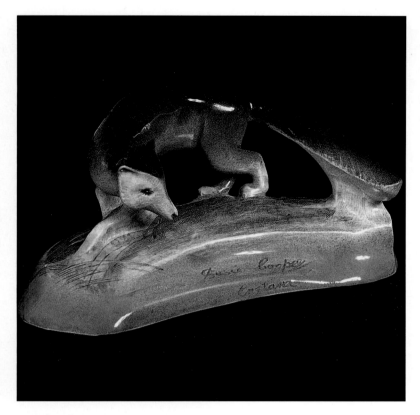

'Fox' was designed in 1937 as a table centre decoration.

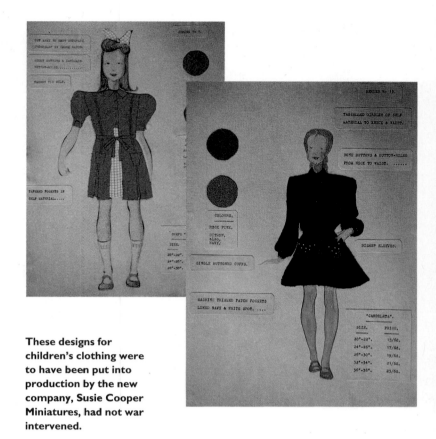

These designs for children's clothing were to have been put into production by the new company, Susie Cooper Miniatures, had not war intervened.

the project had to be shelved. Susie now had to adjust to the radical changes and conditions of wartime.

Government controls over all means of production took effect very quickly in 1939; among the most rigorous were those over 'decoration', which ruled that decorated wares were for export only. Many of the workers were called up for service and the munitions factory at Radway Green, near Stoke-on-Trent, became a particularly big employer of women from the Potteries.

In 1940 Susie was honoured with the Royal Society of Arts Designer for Industry award, the R.D.I. It was a source of great pleasure to Susie that, on hearing of the award, Gordon Forsyth wrote: 'I was delighted to hear that the R.S.A. had the very good sense to confer upon you the very high distinction of the R.D.I. There is no member of that élite body who has made such a one hundred per cent contribution to industrial art as you have.' This was very high praise indeed. Susie Cooper was the first woman R.D.I. and, to this date, she is the only woman from the Potteries to have been honoured in this way. Appreciating the importance of the award, Susie remained fiercely proud of it and always maintained a close relationship with the Royal Society of Arts.

One grim night in May 1942 a fire broke out in the packing house of the Wood's premises and spread to the Susie Cooper Pottery. The damage was very extensive and part of the stock of both companies was destroyed. It took several weeks to secure the buildings and clear away the debris, but finally the decision had to be taken that, instead of struggling to rebuild within the context of wartime shortages and restrictions, the pottery should be closed for the duration of the war.

It was during this period that Susie and Cecil decided to start a family and, in March 1943, their only child, Tim, was born. Despite happiness on the family front, the years of closure of the pottery were turbulent times for Susie. Her nephew Ted Beeson, who had been a great friend and support to her, was killed in action – a devastating loss. Susie busied herself with her young son and her home; the nursery wood panel which she painted for her child at this time tells the tale of happier, more peaceful days.

These personal and professional losses, however, seem finally to have hardened Susie's resolve and sharpened her ambitions. By the end of the war it had become apparent to Cecil Barker that his wife would not be fulfilled unless she could return to work. She was already receiving letters from her overseas agents pleading with her to start up production again and offering help with convincing the authorities of the importance of Susie Cooper Productions in the export markets. But the refurbishment of the Crown Works was certainly an enormous task and the problems were exacerbated by the strict rationing of materials. There were also many other difficulties within the pottery industry itself, but in May 1945 work finally began on the reopening of the Susie Cooper Pottery.

These 'Spiral' wares of 1938 are decorated with the 'Endon' 1417 pattern.

CHAPTER SIX

The vibrant colours and micro-organic motifs proclaim the influence of scientific imagery on these designs (*opposite*) of the immediate post-war years; the group includes 'Starburst' 2068, and 'Chinese feather' 2079.

DESIGNS ON THE FUTURE

1946 – 65

Two 'Quail' shape bowls made as experimental pieces in 1953.

Her own determination and the encouragement of husband and family finally resulted in Susie's reopening of the Crown Works in 1945. Her nephew, Kenneth Cooper, now joined the company. However, rationing of building materials prevented the full refurbishment of the factory for several years, and supplies of all manner of equipment were sporadic or even non-existent. The lithographs which had increasingly become the staple decorative technique of the factory during the pre-war years were used in a limited way after reopening; the old favourites 'Patricia Rose' and 'Dresden Spray' were given new treatments. But the factory stocks of lithographs had been severely damaged in the fire and replacement supplies, even when available, were costly. In response to these difficult circumstances, Susie introduced ranges of hand-painted and aerographed designs. Plant forms dominated the imagery of the new lines, but she now rendered them with a certain organic lightness and optimism, reflecting the style of the period. 'Tree of Life', with its theme of rebirth, seems to capture the essence of the feeling of the years immediately after the war; it remained one of her personal favourites.

Aerographing grew to be a speciality of the Cooper work-force and a number of aerographed wares began to make their way into the company range in the post-war years; this 'Kestrel' coffee set (*below*) includes cups in the 'Doric' shape.

The company stand at the 1947 British Industries Fair was much reduced from its pre-war size; the emphasis of the display is on the painted and aerographed designs.

Susie was now appointed to the selection committee of the 'Britain Can Make It' exhibition, held at the Victoria and Albert Museum, London. The exhibition, organized as a boost to national morale after the war by the Council for Industrial Design (later to become the Design Council), became notorious because the objects shown were largely unavailable on the home market. Instead of having the intended uplifting effect, it came to represent the stringent shortages of the Austerity period. Susie herself showed a range of wares, including a collection of six spiral-decorated plates with extremely elaborate sgraffito, which marked the return of Susie Cooper to ceramic production of the highest quality.

Ironically, Sir Stafford Cripps, President of the Board of Trade, pronounced that the objects on display at the exhibition were of 'wonderful quality and excellent design that will establish for us foreign markets.' The words seem peculiarly misplaced in the light of the problems Susie faced in acquiring the raw materials from the authorities for the refurbishment of the Crown Works to satisfy the demands of eager overseas customers.

The primacy which science came to enjoy during the war years undoubtedly influenced imagery in the decorative arts: microscopic life forms and cell structures were absorbed into the visual language of artists and designers. Susie drew both on these latest forms of imagery and on her own past designs when developing patterns such as 'Starburst'. The massive range of 'Starburst' colourings and variations took polka-dot style patterning to a new level, as painted stars dazzled on the surface of the pottery, bolder and more organic in appearance than the printed stars of the pre-war era.

As soon as it was operative again, the Susie Cooper Pottery was besieged by overseas buyers, as it had been before the war. Susie and her reduced work-force set about decorating everything they could and with whatever materials that were to hand. It is probably due to the exceptional circumstances of this period that some rather unusual pieces, both in decoration and form, occasionally turn up in the United States and Canada. The wildly scrolled, hand-painted forms of designs, such as 'Pear in Pompadour', Susie later described as a form of self-indulgence.

The war had introduced people in the Potteries to many new and varied jobs outside the traditional employment of the region, and the migration of workers out of the industry frequently led to major supply problems: 'The industry was in a state of turmoil.

You might be waiting for cups for all your orders. You just couldn't run the factory with that state of affairs,' Susie later remembered. The supplies and quality of earthenware blanks from Wood's had become less acceptable for her high standards, and labour shortages and unpredictable supplies of materials affected production. By this time it was becoming apparent that the industry would have to offer incentives to entice workers back to the pottery factories. One such incentive was the gradual erosion of the practice of piece-work. Susie found that such changes affected the profitability of certain designs; something as apparently basic as a handle now became much more costly to produce. The 'Kestrel' cover dish, for instance, was one of the victims of the new working conditions. This much-acclaimed piece needed three handles, which meant that it was no longer commercially viable. Instead, Susie produced the covered 'Scallop' dish with one handle.

Ever pragmatic in the face of poor supplies, Susie decided that she would set up production of the wares herself; typically, she had a very clear idea about how to go about it. She later recalled that people had, from the very beginning of her career, told her that her work should be on china because of the high quality of her designs. But it was not just her aspirations that brought her to china, but also the tastes of the post-war buying public. There was a distinct feeling of optimism about the future and of looking forward to better things. In this context, the addition of bone china to the range was a logical progression for Susie, as her aim had always been the pursuit of ever higher standards of quality and utility. Bone china provided her with a fresh opportunity to exercise her exacting standards and Susie reflected in her new designs the optimism about the future which fuelled so much of the vigour of the immediate post-war years. Responsive to changes in the markets, she now planned a dramatic development for her productions.

This unique 14-inch plaque (*above*), with aerographed and painted decoration, was specially made for a family member in the late nineteen-forties.

These patterns (*opposite*) – 'Tulip in Pompadour' 2180 (*above* and *below top left*), 'Pear in Pompadour' 2181 (*below*, the tureen) and the scrolling plaque – were described by Susie Cooper as 'Letting my hair down!'

In June 1950 it was announced in the trade press that Susie Cooper had acquired the china manufacturing business known as Jason China Co. Ltd., which was then renamed Susie Cooper China Ltd. Despite its renaming, however, the compact factory was more often than not referred to as 'Jason' by everyone within the pottery industry. The original company had made small items – reasonably priced cups, saucers and plates, for a relatively down-market clientèle. Susie believed that she could quite easily improve the quality of the output to her exacting standards. As it turned out, this was to take a little longer than she had hoped.

Nevertheless, she was delighted by the first trial pieces which she took home for her own use. The lightness and delicacy of the bone china, she felt, complemented her designs perfectly. Cecil gradually moved into the business full-time, giving up his architectural work and learning the china production process from scratch. He oversaw the Jason site, reorganizing and adding to the original building.

The name 'Quail' was given to the first range of bone china wares that went into production, reflecting the lightness and delicacy of the quail's egg. Even now, many collectors claim that the 'Quail' bone china is the lightest and finest they have known. The shape of the wares is almost impossibly graceful and fine, with sweeping curves and finials. The cover dish of the range continued the functional tradition of the 'Kestrel' in having a cover which doubled as a dish in its own right.

Late in 1950, Susie was approached to furnish the table-ware for the Royal Pavilion at the Festival of Britain exhibition, to be held the following year. She was also put in charge of the crockery requirements of a reception to be held by the Royal Designers for Industry on 7 November 1950. Although the Jason china business was still at a development stage, Susie was certainly not going to refuse the prestigious commission from the body she admired so much. The designs which she produced for the reception must surely count among her most technically accomplished. The sgraffito 'Lion and Unicorn' decorations are of astonishing complexity and embellished with hand-painted gold detailing. Susie later recalled that she, Alice and Nora repeatedly worked late into the night to complete the 40 place-settings.

Unfortunately, the order deadline was so tight that the wells of some of the saucers did not fit the cups perfectly. Princess

The 'Quail' shape coffee pot, with the 'Scrolls' C653 pattern, was one of the main designs of the early fifties from the new china company.

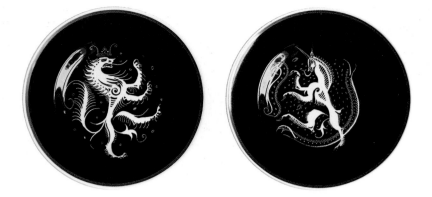

Elizabeth, the guest of honour at the reception, noticed this, much to Susie's embarrassment; the great Miss Cooper was fallible and human after all. The Princess was presented with a number of plates as a gift, and the faulty saucers were quickly replaced. The 'Lion and Unicorn' pieces later made an appearance at the Festival of Britain itself, with the addition of cocktail service dishes, ashtrays, flower vases and service plates. Also used at the Festival was 'Gold bud' C163. The Homes and Gardens section of the exhibition presented the 'Quail' range to the public for the first time, and patterns such as the pink 'Astral' C12, 'Sea anemone' C7–10 and 'Vine leaf' C16 were also given considerable prominence in the exhibition and in the accompanying review in *The Studio Year Book* for 1951–52.

Another special service was ordered for the opening of the 'Exhibition of Exhibitions' at the Royal Society of Arts in May 1951. In response, Susie produced her 'Astral' design in one of her favourite colours, Sèvres blue; this was entered in the pattern book as C156 and was exclusive to the R.S.A. The design had to be fired twice, once for the aerographed and sgraffito decoration, and then for the gold printed stars. This made the design more costly but Susie felt that its sumptuous decoration made it an appropriate

These 'Lion and Unicorn' wares (*above left*) were produced for the Royal Pavilion at the Festival of Britain, 1951.

Another Festival of Britain exhibit was the 'Sea Anemone' set (*above*), with sgraffito decoration in mahogany brown.

Susie Cooper's personal copy of the Royal Society of Arts plaque of 1954 (*left*); the plaque, a technical *tour de force*, was produced on behalf of the Royal Designers for Industry to commemorate the bicentenary of the R.S.A. The decoration is purely freehand, since no sketching or marking could be made on the aerographed surface.

A set of salmon-pink wares (*left*) in the 'Raised spot' C501 pattern; the raised on-glaze spots were the incarnation in china form of the earthenware 'Polka dot' pattern.

This vase (*right*) is embellished with painted and sgraffito decoration.

'Quail' shape tea-ware (*below*) with in-glaze designs; in the early nineteen-fifties such designs were thought to be too advanced for the taste of the market, although they gave Susie Cooper much personal pleasure.

response to an R.S.A. commission. The 'Astral' service saw many years of service and now, in its reduced state, is still preserved by the society. The Royal Designers for Industry organization provided yet another commission for Susie when, in 1954, a plaque was ordered to commemorate the bicentenary of the Royal Society of Arts. The 12-inch plaque took Susie to her limits in terms of artistic and technical expertise, and it was decorated entirely by Susie herself. The sgraffito decoration and lettering on the plaque had to be produced without any guide-lines, as these would have spoiled the aerographed surface. A very steady hand and close concentration were required.

Susie's designs at this time were created mainly for bone china. She was hugely motivated by her new medium and fresh patterns emerged very rapidly. The motifs of her best-known designs were adapted for use on the new lines; the polka dots, for instance, now took the form of enamel spots in relief, delicately covering the surface of the wares. The printed stars of the pre-war earthenware period were also revived for bone china in the form of glittering diapers in gold, or in banded or aerographed interiors.

After her first experiences in china design and production, Susie had come to feel that the china wares allowed for more detailed and costly decoration, and so she set about perfecting her in-glaze techniques. The in-glaze process she used was particularly complex and difficult to execute. The designs were a series of intertwining floral lithographic outline prints with durable colour finishes in bright pink, yellow, green and black. The pieces were then fired again, the decoration dropping into the glaze. Susie felt that the patterns were stylish enough to warrant the cost of the

Interior displays at Harrod's (*above left* and *right*), *c.* 1955; the central figurine is that of the 'Queen Eleanor' trial piece; the table setting of 'Quail' shape wares is in the 'Romanesque' C815 pattern.

three firings that they took to produce. The in-glaze wares have an illusive quality, in their deep colourful pools of pattern, in the pure white of the body and in the sparkling glaze. These in-glaze experiments, unfortunately, were ahead of their time and remained mostly trials. Samples sent to South Africa, Susie remembered with sadness, returned without orders: 'It wasn't understood, it was too different.' The quest to have in-glaze decoration on china accepted remained one of her main aims in later career. Unfortunately, it became one of her few pieces of unfinished business.

With the ending of post-war restrictions on the ceramics industry in 1952, the Susie Cooper businesses could now build on their strengths and enter a new phase of development. Around 1955 Susie started to work on some larger bone china pieces; bulbous lamp bases and vases with and without serpentine moulding were added to the range. A set of bone china figures of famous kings and queens was planned; one figure exhibited in 1955 was that of Queen Eleanor of the Crosses, a 12-inch high figure very much in Susie's own style, but this did not reach production. At least two other figures were modelled, one of a fierce-looking bull and the other of a seated Chinese man, but these never got beyond trial castings.

Elegant classical designs now began to emerge from the factory, such as 'Pomme d'or', 'Corinthian' and the new 'Fluted' shape. The advertising for 'Pomme d'or' took up the classical allusions: 'According to mythology, Paris awarded the Golden Apple to Venus as a token of beauty. Ever since, the Golden Apple has been a symbol of admiration.' A new sales venue, the Blackpool Gifts

The cost of extended production of the 'Pomme d'or' C824 pattern (*right*) proved prohibitive because of its use of gold, even though early hand-painting was eventually replaced by lithography.

A set of wares (*below left*) decorated with 'Assyrian' motif C1010. Boxed sets of wares (*below right*) were introduced around 1957.

and Fancy Goods Fair of 1957, provided the opportunity for the introduction of a new range of boxed items. The exquisite packaging for these wares was designed by Susie herself, opening up yet another area of sales for the company.

During the post-war period the potentially harmful effects of certain metals used in glazes began to be studied. The implications of toxic metal release, as it became known, sent ripples of concern through the ceramics industry. Scandinavian countries in particular desired much lower levels of toxic metal release, and so British manufacturers had to introduce more stringent methods of produc-

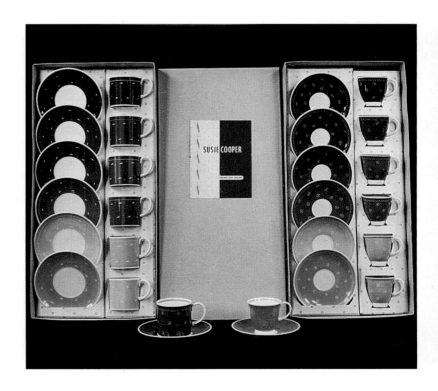

tion if they wished to export to countries with more rigorous limits than at home. On-glaze decoration was one of the problem areas, and so under-glaze decoration had to be considered as an alternative. In any case, on-glaze decoration was more susceptible to damage during general use and especially from strong detergents and dishwashers, the increasing use of which during the nineteen-fifties further encouraged the move to the under-glaze method. This change affected the style of decoration considerably.

Under-glaze colours are inherently less brilliant in hue than on-glaze enamels, and so the change at this period to more organically inspired colouring appears not to have been solely driven by matters of taste. However, Susie's own colour palette, established in the nineteen-thirties and characterized by its array of muted tones, accommodated these enforced changes quite easily. There was one notable change in decorating technique: the appearance of solid banding. Wash-banding and shading, which had been staple techniques of the Susie Cooper Pottery in previous years, were not possible on biscuit pottery, and so solid opaque bands provide the finish to designs such as 'Ferndown'. One aspect of the business, though, which remained steadfast throughout the changes was Susie's commitment to the highest standards of work. The ranges of under-glaze designs, such as 'Blue fern' or 'Highland grass', bear close scrutiny as detailed and controlled examples of handpainting. Tragically for Susie, her progress was to be dramatically halted once again.

During the evening of 21 March 1957, the Crown Works was once more devastated by fire. Fortunately, nobody was injured, but the report of the fire describes the terrible scene of fire-fighters caught in a hail of red-hot splinters of asbestos, glass and pottery. In her personal scrapbook Susie described the fire as 'dreadful' and 'which put us out of business for almost a year … the effects of which were incalculable'. The source of the fire remained a mystery.

The scene at the Crown Works immediately after the fire of March 1957.

Although the warehouse was destroyed and with it a huge quantity of wares destined for home and export markets, the decorating area was saved by the fire brigade. Rebuilding took nearly a year and only small orders not requiring the use of warehouse space were fulfilled by the company. Only 15 designs were entered in the earthenware pattern book between January 1957 and August of the following year; a similar number of china patterns were noted. At the Blackpool fair of 1958 it was announced in the trade press that, 'Patterns introduced last year are only now going into production, and in many cases first deliveries are being made at this time. The Company regards the 1958 Fair as providing an opportunity to introduce the new reduced range to buyers.'

The tenacity that had always marked the life and work of Susie Cooper was once again fully in evidence as she struggled to make up for the losses in the fire. She later described how she summoned up the energy to cope with the crisis: 'If it's something you want to do, you find the strengths and the means to do it, the desire to do it.' And the massive success of the few designs that were produced at this time, such as 'Black Fruit' and the new and radical 'Can' shape, spurred Susie on to new initiatives to counter the problems of a reduced rate of growth. Since starting her bone china manufacture, she had wanted to produce dinner ware in addition to the coffee and tea wares. 'I wanted to do in the china field what I had done in the earthenware field … make dinner ware … I wanted to make china more accessible, nice china, china with style and quality, and that people could buy and use.' The Jason factory, even though it had been extended on either side under Susie and Cecil, still did not provide enough space for the demands of dinner ware production. The answer to the problem was quickly found by Susie.

The Plant family of pottery manufacturers had been acquaintances of Susie for many years and had a tunnel oven which was not used to its full capacity ('I thought, what's the good of building another factory when there's one up the road just waiting, and so it was a mutual arrangement.'). In December 1958 the Susie Cooper companies merged with R.H. and S.L. Plant, to form the Tuscan Holdings group. One important aspect of the merger was that the individuality of the production and separate running of the two factories was assured. China production was transferred to the Plant's premises and the Jason factory sold off. The Crown Works continued as the centre of Susie Cooper Productions, and she invested in its future and her independence by buying the premises from Wood & Sons. Indeed the close, amicable relationship with Wood's had been slowly changing, as the demands of bone china production and the reduction of the earthenware market took effect, ending in the eventual phasing out of earthenware decoration. The unique identity of the Susie Cooper Pottery was further enhanced by the refurbishment of the Crown Works inside and out to plans by Cecil and Susie. These included the painting of the Susie Cooper Pottery section of the building in a special cream colour, also extended to the window casements, to give a clean, fresh look to the premises.

Susie Cooper designs were regularly commended by the Council of Industrial Design, and her work was now consistently illustrated in *The Studio Yearbook*. As the earthenware side of the business was wound down, Susie concentrated her efforts on the bone china production. The last earthenware pattern entry is dated 30 July 1964, and production ceased altogether soon after this.

By the mid sixties, however, the Plant family, Susie's partners in the Tuscan group, began to be concerned over their liability for death duties and the financial stability of the family. When Wedgwood made a take-over approach in 1966, the offer of participation and shares in the ceramics giant was too attractive to resist, although Susie would have preferred to remain independent.

Ranges of china and earthenware of the late nineteen-fifties and early sixties: 'Rex' shapes, including a 'Scallop' dish, in the 'Gooseberry' under-glaze design (*above left*); the much acclaimed 'Can' shape in 'Corinthian' C2056 (*above right*); the 'Rex' shape in 'Hazelwood' 2375 (*below left*); another set of 'Can' in 'Sunflower' C2002 (*below right*).

'Classic Vista' 990, one of the most popularly admired of all Susie Cooper designs, made its appearance in the pattern books in 1959.

CHAPTER SEVEN

'Black fruit' (*opposite*) was first
introduced by Susie Cooper in
the nineteen-fifties and remained
a very successful design during her
Wedgwood years.

WEDGWOOD

1966–80

In March 1966 Susie Cooper Ltd., as part of Tuscan Holdings, was absorbed into the Wedgwood Group. It appeared for a time that the change would benefit Susie greatly. The designer believed she would have the considerable resources of the huge company at her disposal and could concentrate on utilizing them without the distraction of factory management duties. In other words, she could finally get down to designing ceramics and continuing her experiments.

Kenneth Cooper was made a director of both Susie Cooper Ltd. and also of William Adams & Sons Ltd., another member of the Wedgwood Group, the idea being that the two companies should be run side by side. The company showroom was closed and a joint one for Susie Cooper and William Adams opened. Arthur Bryan, then managing director of Wedgwood, announced, 'It is particularly satisfying to report that Susie Cooper has agreed to continue to work with the new organization. We all look forward with great interest to her participation in design matters.'

It was not just the prospect of working with the eminent Susie Cooper which attracted Wedgwood, but also the prospect of acquiring her highly skilled work-force and the ranges of existing designs, including the much acclaimed 'Can' shape. Another exciting line was the 'Contrast' series, worked in solid aerographed colour set off by the pure whiteness of the china body. 'Contrast' was another example of Susie's efforts to reach larger markets; its simple decoration reduced cost and meant that it could be sold at about half the price of a design such as 'Assyrian'. Such innovations by Susie also coincided with a move within Wedgwood to attract the extensive youth market and to modernize the main company's output. Unfortunately for this initiative, the price of the wares still remained relatively high.

Nevertheless, this period saw Susie in buoyant mood and, very much with an eye on the future, she began to produce a range of designs with space-age titles such as 'Saturn', 'Andromeda' and 'Mercury', which she named in her notes 'The Planet Series'. Simplicity is the key element in these designs, with small boxed motifs arranged in a clean strip of colour. The 'Nebula' pattern continued Susie's experiments in the juxtaposition of matt and gloss decoration; in this design, the gloss motif is a cosmic swirl of breath-taking audacity. Her colour palette began to reflect her growing interest in deep saturated colours, but, as usual, there is an illusive quality about her use of them.

A visit to London was never very popular with Susie. She disliked the bustle and the rapid pace of life, but a tour around the

The 'Can' shapes of a revolutionary year, 1968; cosmic swirls in matt aerograph and covercoat in 'Nebula' C2135.

A set of elegant space-age design ('Contrast') in covercoat.

This 'Harlequinade' set, with its vigorous colour matching, was the outcome of the search by Wedgwood for a more immediately contemporary image; the colours of Op Art had a clear influence on Susie Cooper at this time.

The newly popular 'Can' shape, however, still lent itself easily to more traditional patterns: 'Persia' C2019.

city in the latter part of 1967 did produce some startling results. After a visit to some of the key areas of 'swinging' London, under the guidance of Sir Paul Reilly of the Design Council, she was inspired on her return to the Potteries to produce a series of quite remarkable designs. 'Carnaby Daisy' is quite clearly a direct response to the visit: its Pop Art flower motif made use of the fashionable graphic imagery of the day. The multi-coloured 'Harlequinade', particularly when seen as a set, is another startling design of this period. It employs vivid, clashing colours in lava lamp blobs which seem to merge and transform in colour and shape.

'Ashmun' C2206 in covercoat, 1971, reflected contemporary interest in the imagery and artefacts of Ancient Egypt.

Especially popular in Scandinavian countries, which were then considered pre-eminent in design matters, the appearance of this set does mark yet another stage in the confirmation of Susie's international status.

It is perhaps the unexpected, the quality of sheer surprise in these designs of the sixties which makes them so remarkable. That a designer, herself already in her sixties, could use the fashionable visual vocabulary of the day to such effect is, rightly or wrongly, surprising. Most remarkably, perhaps, Susie succeeded in placing these bold contemporary designs among the ranges of one of the most traditional of fine china manufacturers. Wedgwood at this time certainly had very little that was comparable, apart from some

abstract designs by Eduardo Paolozzi issued, significantly, as a limited edition in 1970. Yet, despite these design triumphs, Susie found it an increasing struggle to push her designs through the corporate structures of Wedgwood and into production.

The decisions of the design selection meetings at Wedgwood were dictated by a volatile market; designs which, it was felt, did not have the potential for extensive sales simply did not get produced. It was reported that in 1969 seventy-five per cent of designs failed to go to the production stage. As well as finding circumstances at Wedgwood increasingly difficult, Susie was also embattled personally. Her husband had been very ill for some time and died in March 1972, a loss which she felt very deeply. Without his staunch sup-

The 'Ashmun' Egyptian theme was continued by Wedgwood to this range of gift-ware (*left*).

These 'Chou', 'Persia' and 'Egyptian' designs (*opposite*), inspired by ancient works of art, were eventually abandoned by Wedgwood, apart from 'Chou' which was produced in limited quantities.

port, progress at Wedgwood proved very arduous. In May of that year Susie resigned from her position as director, as did Kenneth Cooper. She was now to act solely as designer, while her nephew moved elsewhere within the Wedgwood management structure.

In spite of professional frustration – certainly exacerbated by personality clashes with part of the Wedgwood management – Susie still managed to produce a number of very successful designs. 'Corn

A prototype design for 'Corn Poppy'; the series went on to be one of Wedgwood's most successful lines in the late nineteen-seventies and early eighties.

poppy' and 'Charisma', for instance, encouraged her to continue with her many experiments and prototype designs. After her struggles to get table-ware designs into production, Susie now turned her attentions to a range of decorative designs inspired by Persian, Chinese, Ancient Egyptian and Roman art. The results were, quite simply, spectacular. Tragically, only the Chinese 'Chou' design was made in any quantity, while the rest of the range remained a series of exquisite trials.

Recognition and acclaim for her work was now widespread; this was the period when she began to interest serious collectors and students of ceramic design. In 1978 Wedgwood supported a retrospective of her work at Sanderson's in London. A visitors' book from this exhibition was filled with admiring comments from all over the world, which came as something of a surprise to Susie – she treasured the book until her death.

In the New Year's Honours List of 1979 Susie was awarded the Order of the British Empire, an award made all the more welcome since her contemporary and long-time customer, Queen Elizabeth the Queen Mother, carried out the investiture.

'In hindsight I would have stayed on my own.' These words, spoken by Susie Cooper in recollection of the merger with R.H. and S.L.Plant, emphasize how important complete control over production had always been to her. Her forceful vision necessitated that level of control, and the weakening of her control over the design function ran contrary to everything she held dear. Susie eventually became a victim of circumstances at Wedgwood and of changing markets. Most ironically, she had been made a victim of her own goals.

The economic recession after 1979 wrought havoc with the manufacturing base in Britain. Problems in the market for the multi-national group were magnified in the subsidiary factories. Susie Cooper faced her biggest professional blow when in 1980 her

beloved Crown Works was closed down. The closure was intended to ensure continued work at the Wedgwood headquarters in Barlaston and thus secure the jobs there. For nearly fifty years the Crown Works had been the centre of Susie's life. A perplexed work-force was gathered together and, with very great sadness, told of its fate. Some workers were moved to other jobs in the Wedgwood group, but the rest were made redundant. The closure

of the Crown Works was a matter of great sadness and distress to Susie Cooper, as her workers had invested so much pride and hard work in the company, in many cases for their whole working lives. Some of those present on the day of closure recall the intensity of her fury. For many years Susie held on to the belief that one day she might reopen the Crown Works. Despite all that had happened, Susie Cooper was not completely discouraged.

'Bird' plaque in experimental reactive glazes, 1978.

CHAPTER EIGHT

White Monkey, a 'Seed Painting'
(*opposite*); the unusual subject-matter
and technique of these works received
a mixed reception in 1991.

EPILOGUE

1 9 8 0 – 9 5

With the closure of the Crown Works, Susie was faced with the choice of either moving to the Wedgwood design premises at Barlaston or to another location within the Wedgwood Group. John Ryan, managing director of William Adams & Sons, now part of Wedgwood, was able to persuade her to continue her work and to base herself at the factory premises in Furlong Road, Tunstall. Adams & Sons was respected in the Potteries as a high-quality earthenware manufacturer and, after one lengthy discussion with John Ryan, Susie decided there was a basis for collaboration.

Ryan did an excellent job of welcoming Susie to the works. A large office was created for her by knocking two smaller rooms into one. The furniture from her office at the Crown Works was installed to create a familiar working environment for Adams' new, honoured designer. The considerable trouble to which the Adams director went to accommodate Susie was a mark of his personal and professional esteem for her. 'She deserved it, she had great potential and a fighting spirit', he later recalled. Ryan also kept a close personal watch on Susie's experiments, which were helped by another part of the Wedgwood Group, Precision Studios, especially in the application of various lustres to covercoat.

Another area of experimentation for Susie at this time was the use of 'reactive' glazes. These were applied to covercoat and, when fired, underwent a chemical process. Susie recalled later, 'They (Adams) did a tremendous lot to improve and develop the body they had … I was always preaching to them about the weight of the body.' Ultimately, Susie was very satisfied with the Adams Micratex range, a clear sign of her approval being that she used it herself at home from day to day. The Micratex body, developed by Jocelyn Adams and introduced in 1983, had the larger particles in the clay

These experimental lustre pieces were developed for Adams' gift-ware ranges.

reduced in number, making a body two to three times stronger than normal. The development of the higher durability Micratex body echoed the kind of experiments in quality and utility that Susie herself had always undertaken. Roller and curvex printing for biscuit decoration was viewed by both John Ryan and Susie as very suitable for her designs; this was a development of rubber-stamp printing ideal for the economical mass-production of simple patterns. The 'Meadowlands' and 'Inspiration' designs were now produced for sale in Boots, the high-street chemist, and in Tesco, one of Britain's largest supermarket chains, respectively. Susie was delighted, having always been concerned to make her work available to as wide a buying public as possible. To coincide with her eightieth birthday, Adams launched the 'Daisy' design, to much critical acclaim.

A catalogue of the Adams range in the mid nineteen-eighties contained a proud record of Susie's work for the company: 'Two of the patterns have been designed by Susie Cooper O.B.E., R.D.I., doyenne of British pottery designers and senior member of the Wedgwood Group's team of resident designers. "Florida" is a vivacious up-date of a pattern which she created in the nineteen-thirties and "Blue Haze" is a 1984 original.'

A whole string of prototypes in Micratex ware illustrates the interest Susie had at this period in the production of fine-body oven-to-table crockery. There are dozens of quite remarkable prototypes at the Wedgwood Museum, a testament to the agelessness of her talents and skills and to the belief John Ryan had in her work.

The ground had thus been prepared for what should have been an extremely successful and fruitful working relationship between Adams and Susie. However, a series of problems beset their projects and eventually brought their cooperation to an end. John Ryan had proposed the use of Susie's name in the back stamp for her designs to promote jointly the distinguished designer and the products of the company. But this use of the back stamp was blocked by Wedgwood management, claiming that the name was too prestigious for use on the 'lowly' earthenware body. That Susie Cooper, with her exacting standards, was proud to have her name on the wares should really have been sufficient reason to use it in that context.

'Tiffany Polka Dot' (*below left*) recalls the simple motifs which made Susie Cooper famous in the nineteen-thirties; even 'Florida' (*below right*), though entirely of its time, is a re-work of a design originally created fifty years earlier.

Although he exercised considerable influence over the design of the Adams production, Ryan now began to feel that Susie's ability and potential was being squandered by the Wedgwood Group. He later admitted with some sadness, 'We could have utilized her talents better.' Someone as forceful as Susie Cooper, however, was probably destined to feel frustrated; anything less than total commitment and integrity on the part of others was unacceptable to her. Even the influence of allies such as John Ryan and the support of her family could not prevent Susie from feeling that she now needed to break away from the increasingly frustrating strictures of the industry. She had in fact reached a turning point: a decision to break with the Potteries and move to the Isle of Man.

Though often viewed as a kind of official retirement, the move to the Isle of Man in fact heralded a new phase in Susie Cooper's work. Peaceful retirement would for most people be quite natural at the age of 84 and after 64 years work. Instead, Susie launched herself into a whole range of projects. With her son Tim she set about making a home in a huge five-storey Victorian house which looked on to a garden square. She became deeply involved in her new environment, campaigning to have the square restored and listed for preservation. The five-storey home, a place for 'vertical living' as she termed it, increasingly became a place of pilgrimage for journalists, researchers and students. Widespread attention was focused on her work by a variety of events, beginning with the major retrospective exhibition at the Victoria & Albert Museum in 1987. Organized by Ann Eatwell of the museum, the exhibition was hugely successful and attended by many thousands of visitors from all over the world. It was beginning to dawn on this supremely modest designer that her work was of considerable importance. In the same year, Susie found herself sixty-five glorious years later once again at the portals of the Royal College of Art. This time, instead of turning her back on the college in favour of work in the Potteries, she accepted an Honorary Doctorate.

Susie's work into the later nineteen-eighties and into the nineties continued to be sensitive to the moods and the styles of the time. The environmental issues which have come to the fore in recent years and concern for the preservation of nature, for

Rabbit, a 'Seed Painting' made for Joy Couper.

instance, inspired her to use natural, muted tones. These concerns lie at the heart of her 'Seed Paintings', which are made of the very stuff of nature.

She had tentatively begun such works in the nineteen-seventies before she left the Crown Works, but the 'Seed Paintings', as she called them, had had to wait until her retirement to be resumed. Although these works at first seem far removed from her ceramic designs, they are in fact simply another expression of her vision. She said of this phase of her work, 'I hope it will be accepted as a new art form. Whether it will or not I don't know, but it is to me.'

These pictures are experimental, expressive renderings of natural forms, the subject-matter most dear to her. But here form and content are united in that the works themselves are made from natural objects – the seeds. The technique of collage is used to achieve great subtlety and decorative sophistication. Seeds were chosen for their colouring or pattern and were also often applied individually. Once again, Susie's search for the refinement and development of techniques is evident. Her wood-panel paintings, which had adorned her trade stands at the British Industries Fairs and her own home, were another starting-point for the 'Seed Paintings', in the swirling lines now painstakingly applied in seed and grain.

In later life, Susie had become critical of much that she saw around her, sadly remarking that people did not actually make very much anymore and, instead, concerned themselves with the abstractions of money-making. The 'Seed Paintings' can be seen within this context, as wilfully labour-intensive works, quite at odds with immediate fashion. They may also perhaps be read as signposts for the future.

Textile design again appeared on Susie Cooper's agenda when a representative of Twilley's, a textile firm, saw her 'Seed Paintings' in an exhibition. As a result, she was asked if she would produce a range of tapestry designs. Susie's response was to produce a series of simplified animal motifs. Unfortunately, the sets were only available for a short time before Twilley's went into receivership.

Susie's ninetieth-birthday celebrations were marked by a whole range of products and events. Among these were two books and a 'Leaping Deer' figure modelled in porcelain by Susie and made at the Isle of Man's Shebeg Pottery. Susie even set her hand to her long-time ambition of modelling bookends. But the figures, which Susie wanted to be produced in red clay, as 'Lummox' had been, had to be made in white earthenware; it seems to have been too great a problem for the modern industry to make them in her preferred material, which recalled the highly individual sculpted triumphs of the nineteen-twenties.

A late appearance of the 'Kestrel' design: this 1988–89 version has a design of pink fern.

In her felt 'pictures' of 1992, Susie Cooper ruefully acknowledged the popularity of the forms and colours of her early geometric designs; it was planned that these re-creations should be issued in kit form.

The opening (*opposite*) of the retrospective exhibition at London's Victoria and Albert Museum in 1987 brought together Doris Gleaves (bander), Susie Cooper herself, and Nora Dobbs (freehand painter).

The restoration and redecoration of old furniture was another interest of these late years. Modest second-hand pieces were turned into articles of great beauty and excitement with scrolling floral designs. One headboard is adorned with languid swans, while another is decorated with an impossibly sumptuous bloom over a little sleeping face. Old moulds of her wares began to be reworked, while she began to develop a modern-day studio range.

During her life Susie made relatively few radio or television appearances and gave few interviews. She was essentially a person who always looked forward; even when using motifs or designs from earlier periods of her long career, she would always rework them in some way. She refused to dwell on the past, and although she did reluctantly recognize the present-day popularity of the Gray's geometric designs, she still maintained that this was due to the fact that fashion had dictated that her early work should receive a disproportionate amount of publicity.

The 'Pottery Ladies' television films of 1985 examined the work of Susie Cooper, Charlotte Rhead and Clarice Cliff, but in 1994, Susie on her ninety-second birthday received the accolade of a short film devoted to her work alone, made for the Channel 4 television station. Susie was exceptionally interested in this project because it attempted to look at her work beyond the Art Deco era. The film did show what a remarkable woman Susie was – hard-working, modest and quite simply inspirational. In an interview for BBC Radio Stoke in 1992, Susie explained why she continued to work: 'I feel I can't live in today's world on yesterday's terms. Times are changing all the time, and I don't want to sit around and wait for death. As long as I can do something, I think it is foolish not to do it.'

Susie Cooper died on 28 July 1995. Right up to her last days she spent her time experimenting and campaigning for perfection in all things. She also became very interested in the plans for the writing of this book. She wanted as many people as possible to see her designs, so that the development of her life's work would be recorded and her very great influence assured.

A late interest in Susie Cooper's life was the refurbishment of old, usually modest furniture, which she decorated with scrolling floral designs.

PATTERN LISTS

The pattern lists given below are divided into four sections: the Gray's period (1923–29); the matt glazes (from 1932); the earthenware designs (1929–64); the china designs (1951–85). Unfortunately, the actual pattern books of A.E. Gray & Co. are missing, making a complete listing impossible, and hitherto unknown designs are discovered regularly. Ascribing designs of this period to Susie Cooper is fraught with problems, particularly as it is not certain whether or not she was the sole designer during her years at Gray's. The earliest pattern currently believed to be by Susie Cooper at Gray's is numbered 2866 and the last is thought to be in the region of 8600. Dates for the Gray's wares are approximate only and have been arrived at by examination of trade press records and archive documents.

The earthenware lists are taken from the pattern books of Susie Cooper Productions. Designs were given 'E' numbers, indicating an earthenware pattern. The prefix was not much used after E500. The letter 'S' used as a prefix denotes the more costly designs with silver lustre. Pattern numbering begins at E50; this was designed to hide the newness of the business in its early days. Dates were not entered next to a design until the late nineteen-fifties and so the dating of the designs here must be regarded as approximate; it is derived largely from comments by Susie, advertising and from contemporary articles in the trade press. When dating any examples of Susie Cooper pottery, it must be remembered that many designs were produced over several years, even decades. A pot in a pattern designed in 1932, for example, may quite easily have been produced later. The pattern marks themselves have been found on a number of occasions to be incorrect and so again care needs to be exercised in evaluating them. Painted marks, applied by the piece-work paintress at speed, can be very difficult to read; this is particularly so in the case of painted numbers 4 and 7 which can look very similar. The impressed marks so often found on the Wood's ware (flat ware in particular) denote when the pottery body was made; for example, 636 denotes a pot manufactured in June 1936. These marks should be read with care as it may have been some time before the pottery was decorated. In the case of Susie Cooper Productions, however, the impressed marks do provide a reasonably accurate date as white ware blanks would usually be ordered as they were needed, and it was not good practice to decorate old pottery.

Many designs by Susie Cooper were never entered into the pattern books. These are chiefly the short order or limited production lines such as: 'Seagull', 'Puck', 'Homestead'; lustre animals – fox, unicorn and lion in blue or tango orange jackets; wall masks of Greta Garbo, Susie herself, the judge, the Chinaman; figures – walking woman, Queen Eleanor, Chinaman, bull; napkin rings modelled as terrier, fox, swan, and so on, at the Crown Works after Susie's originals.

Susie Cooper's shrewd eye for business often led her to sell trial pieces, which are particularly desirable for collectors. The latter must be aware of the increasing number of forgeries on the market; a general guide is that marks on genuine Susie Cooper productions tend to be well-defined and distinct. The quality of the decoration, however, is probably the best guide to authenticity.

To keep the massive listings to a manageable extent, the colour variations of patterns are given as a single entry and the abbreviated list of colours should be read as consecutive pattern number descriptions. For example the entry '70–71 Banding in: o lustre, g lustre' – means that E70 is orange lustre banding and E71 is green lustre banding.

The listing of the patterns on china is taken from Susie Cooper's own pattern book from the late nineteen-fifties, but all other dates are approximate and derived from comments by Susie Cooper, trade press and archive material. Due to a mistake at the factory, numbers 1200–1999 were never used.

ABBREVIATIONS

aero =	aerographed
ag =	apple green
apri =	apricot
aub =	aubergine glaze
b =	blue
bk =	black
bn =	brown
cc =	covercoat
cant =	cantaloupe (orange yellow)
cbn =	chestnut brown
cela =	celadon green
chart =	chartreuse green
chg =	chrome green
chin b =	chinese blue
ey =	egg yellow
fern =	fern green
g =	green
glad g =	gladioli green
gpy =	green pale yellow
gy =	grey
gyb =	grey blue
hbn =	hair brown
in-g =	in-glaze
kb =	kingfisher blue
l =	lilac
lav =	lavender
lg =	longmore green
litho =	lithographic transfer print
M&S o =	Meir & Swan orange
mbn =	mahogany brown
mwg =	matt white glaze
o =	orange
old g =	old gold
on-g =	on-glaze
p =	purple
pbn =	purple brown
pomp =	pompadour (deep red)
r =	red
rbn =	red brown
s pink =	salmon pink
sb =	smoke blue
sbn =	smoke brown
sev =	Sèvres blue
sgraf =	sgraffito decoration
sgy =	silver grey
sy =	silver yellow
t =	tomato red
tang =	tangerine
tgo =	tango
turq =	turquoise
u-g =	under-glaze
v =	violet
y =	yellow

A.E. GRAY & CO. PATTERNS (1923–29)

1923
2866 Simple floral pattern, in r & y, y dontil edge.
1924
5177 Lions, in copper lustre scrolls & spots.
5241 Simple flower diaper in copper lustre, wave border at top.
1925
5365 Gloria Lustre, swirling stylized floral in r, p, l, lustre outlined in gold.
5368 Gloria Lustre, simple central flower in p, b, r.
5373 Gloria Lustre, gold-lined, o, p, b fruit ruby lustre.
5399 Gloria Lustre, p, b & ruby floral, outline gold.
1927
7257 Vine & key border in silver lustre.
7275 Oranges, stylized border.
1928
7456 Tulip & flowers, in bn, bk, maroon, y.
7668 Acorns, print & enamel.
7670 Banded, wide in r, y, g with bk lines.
7671 Golden catkin, print & enamel.
7714 Almond blossom.
7742-7743 Quadrupeds, nursery ware animal subjects inc. horse, lamb, pig, cow, deer, print & enamel.
7834 This is the House that Jack Built, nursery ware, print & enamel.
7872 Simple floral edge spray.
7885 Iris, print & enamel.
7912 Lupin, simple stylized flowers.
7924 Stylized floral, wavy flower-heads on y glaze.
7940 Vertical wavy bands with spots y, o, bk.
7953 Tulip & large flower-heads, filled behind in bk.
7956 Floral, bold flower-heads on y glaze.

7960 Moon & Mountains, overlapping zig-zags & circles in bk, r, b, g, y.
7996 Bold brush-stroke floral.
1929
8071 Cubist, geometric overlapping squares in b, g, y, r & bk, with r line to edge.
8085 Daffodils, print & enamel.
8086 Purple crocus, print & enamel.
8097 Geometric arced spikes & circles, r, bk, y, gy.
8099 Geometric overlapping circles, r, b, y, bk, g.
8112 Crocus, print & enamel, g scallop border to edge.
8127 Geometric overlapping triangles in bn, y, bk, r, g.
8133 Jagged points, in g lustre with lustre marbling.
8286 Layebands, y & pink bands.
8321 Pastoral, animal subjects, inc. deer, hound & hare.
8330 Vertical stripes with dontil edge in r, b, g, y, bk.
8374 Hawaiian, simple stylized fruit & leaves, in g, y, o.
8408 Thistle, simple, hand-painted in g & pink.
8494 Blue lupins, tall simple floral motifs.
8554 Persian bird, stylized swirling bird in silver lustre.

MATT GLAZES (1932 ONWARDS)
The matt glaze items listed below are taken from the pattern books of Susie Cooper. The designs listed are for a mixed range of 'studio' wares designed from 1932 onwards. These include tube-lined, under-glaze (in-glaze) decoration and carved designs. All numbers were given the prefix 'M' to denote matt glaze. There appears to have been some overlapping of numeration, as some designs were given 'E' numbers as well as 'M' numbers. Matt glaze items from a later period than those listed were given reference numbers without prefix: these are believed to refer to the shape rather than the pattern.

60 Stylized leaves, y, apri & bns, vertical pointed leaves with oval leaf between.
61 Peacock feathers & spots, cross-hatched top.
62 Stylized leaves, in copper, apri, y, dk bn.
63 Stylized leaves, in g, apri, dk bn, copper.
64 Stylized floral with leaves.
65 Vertical wavy line border & ovals with wavy base.
66 Large vertical leaves, with wavy border to top.
67 Large vertical leaves with spots, in g, bn, apri.
68 Large vertical leaves, alternate g, pink with apri.
69 Vertical strip of loops in g.
70 Horizontal leaves, cross-hatched edge.
71 Not used.
72 Orchids, stylized floral in pink, y, g & bns.
73 Vertical stylized leaves, alternate colours.
74 Orchids, stylized flower-head curved back inwards.
75 Wavy lines at base with stylized flower-head at top.
76 Tulip-style flower-head & leaves.
77 Vertical flower-heads, vertical wavy spikes.
78 Large wavy leaves.
79 Orchids, colour variation.
80 Bold stylized leaves.
81 Orchids, colour variation & simplified leaves in b.
82 Vertical ovals, in b & bn with wavy spikes.
83 Vertical ovals, as 82 with gy glaze.
84 Stylized leaves.
85 Stylized motifs with wavy leaves, gy glaze.
86 Vertical pointed leaves with oval leaf between, as 60, with gy glaze.
87 Stylized leaves, in copper, apri, y, dark bn, gy glaze.
88 Orchids, as 74 with gy glaze.
89 Wavy lines, as 75 in black.
90 Large vertical leaves, as 66 with gy glaze.
91 Stylized floral with leaves, as 64 with gy glaze.
92 Wavy lines at base, as 75 with gy glaze.
93 Bold stylized leaves, as 80 with cream glaze.
94 Orchids, as 81, in g, y, bk.
95-100 Floral spray carved on fruit tray, in g, gy, gy jade, flame, turq jade, buff.
101 Floral carved, with tooth border, g glaze.
102-106 Floral carved glazes, colours as 95–100.
107-112 Floral panels carved, colours as 95–100.
113-118 Fox in landscape, colours as 95–100.
119-124 Floral panels, as 107 on lamp, colours as 95–100.
125-130 Fox in landscape, as 113 on lamps, colours as 95-100.
131-136 Tube-lined & carved decoration, colours as 95-100.
137-142 Ovals border carved, colours as 95-100.
143-148 Tulip, stylized floral carved, colours as 95-100.
149 Squirrel with landscape, g glaze.
150 Orchids, as 72 with gy glaze.
151 Wavy lines, as 75 in bs & bns with gy.
152 Stylized hatched leaf, with gy glaze.
153 Stylized floral multi-leaf carved g glaze.
154 Squirrel, as 149 colour variation.
155 Tulip, carved turq glaze.
156-157 Large spot with stems.
158 Horizontal leaves, as 70 colour variation.
159 Tulip head & leaves, as E402 lamp design.
160 Stylized floral, in b, g, y.
161 Horizontal leaves, as 70 colour variation.
162 Orchids, as 72 b & bn with gy glaze.
163-164 Matt glaze, b decoration.
165-168 Stylized floral multi-leaf, colour glaze gy, g, buff, b.
169 Stylized scroll (shrimp) carved, flame glaze.
170-174 As 169, various colours.

175 Orchid, carved with flame glaze.
176-180 Orchid, various colour glazes.
181 Swirls & lines, apri, bn & bn crayon, aub.
182 Floral, in u-g colours.
183 Tube-lined scrolling, in bk with pink glaze.
184 Chevrons, tube-lined in bk, bn lines, pink glaze.

THE EARTHENWARE DESIGNS (1929–64)

George Street & Chelsea Works

October 1929

50 Banding, y, b, bk, chg.
51 Banding, y, ey, bk, tgo.
52 Geometric, bk, gy, pale y, jade, p.
53 Geometric, bk, gy, y, ey, t.
54 Geometric, bk, ivory, fawn, gold.
55 Tulips, t, ey, b, leaves in g, gy semi-circles.
56 Carnation border, b, jade, gy, ey & t spots.
57 Banding, p, g, tgo, g lines between.
58 Banding, bk, t, y, tr, bk, with g lines between.
59 Geometric, on Grecian bowl.
60 Tulips, t, leaves pbn, pale y, gy & bk, wavy line at edge.
61 Tulips, ey & pale y, leaves gy, b, chg, chg band dontils.
62 Floral, t, y, leaves bk & pale y.
63 Lily of the valley, pale y, gy, chg & bk.
64 Tulip or fritillary, pink, leaves gy & g.
65 Outlined fruit, b, ey, t, outline in gy.
66 Floral, pale y, t, leaves & stems in bk & g.
67 Floral, in tang with bn centre, ey with t centre, leaves chg & gy.
68 Modernist, bk, t, pale y, ey.
69 Modernist (Linear), in b, bk, pale y, chg, cbn.
70–71 Banding in o lustre, g lustre.
72 Geometric, bk, gy, pale y, t, bands in r & bk.
73 Geometric, bk, jade, gy, pale y.
74 Banding, in pale y, tang, t, bk, g lines between.
75 Design in cbn, chg, bk.
76 Carnation border, as 56, t flower, finish in ey.
77 Fruit in o & y with g leaves & lustre finish.
78 Bluebell on dinner ware, Chelsea.
79 Sheraton Stripe.
80 Design in t, b & bk.
81 Windsor Floral.
82 Banded dinner ware in jade, cbn, golden bn, bk.
83 Banding, ¼" bands, in tgo, cbn, golden bn, bk.
84 Banding, ⅜" bands, in jade, cbn, tgo, golden bn.
85 Banding, ⅜" bands, in tgo, cbn, bk, golden bn.
86 Banding, ⅛" bands, tgo, cbn, golden bn, bk.
87 Floral, in tgo with ey & pale y, cbn centres, g leaves.
88 Modernist, spikes in chg & bk, y square spots.
89 On morning set.
90 Modernist, spikes & spots b, jade, ey, mauve spots.
91 Modernist, sim. to 88 but with the addition of b.
92 Modernist, bk triangular pieces b, y, jade, cbn spots.
93 Ash trays & cheese wedges.
94 Floral spray, in ey, pale y, jade, t, t edge & dash.
95 Graduated banding, in coral, ey, bk, pale y.
96 Bronze chrysanthemums, in r & y, g & bk leaves.
97 Floral, as 62 but tang instead of t.
98 Modernist, bands & spots of b & t, bk semi-circles.
99 Tulip, sim. to 64 in pink & p, leaf & stems in gy.

March 1930

100 Persian, in t, rbn, bk, gy.
101 Design in bk, bn, y, silver.
102 Modernist, spikes & wavy bands in bk, jade, b, y spots.
103 Floral, as 62, flowers y & t instead of t & pale y.
104 Daisy, floral border, t, ey, pale y, pale gold & bn leaves.
105 Floral, slight pattern, spikes & flowers with spots.
106 Graduated bands, in g, leaves rbn, spots ey, p.
107 Graduated bands, in b as 106, leaves g, spots ey.
108 Bronze chrysanthemums, kb, v, mauve, grass in green & sgy.
109 Floral, y, bands in b & g.
110 Geometric, in hbn, gy, y, g on y glaze.
111 Crocus, in kb, l, v.
112 Tulips, in v & l, leaves in chg & g.
113 Marigolds, in t, ey, y, bk & g on white body.
114 Modernist, bk leaves & wavy t crescents & y spots.
115 Tulips, as 61 in chg, v, l, l dontils at edge.
116 Spots in graded sizes, b, y, g & gy, y edge.
117 Graduated bk bands (3), spots in t, b, y & g.
118 Graduated g bands (3), spots in pale y, b, rbn & bk.
119 Oval spots (mussels), in b & y, wavy border in b.
120 Spots, various sizes, in y, t, bk, g band at foot.
121 Modernist, similar to 68, in chg, kb with coral spots.
122 Banding in t & y with bk lines between.
123 String bands (on child's mug), chg & v (3 sets).
124 Modernist, long tail spots, p, g, b, square spots ey.
124a Floral, sponged in ey with a spray of flowers.
125 Geometric, sponged chg, b spots, blocks in r, b, ey, y, bk.
126 Floral, r, b, ey, chg, painted on ey washed surface.
127 String bands, as 123 but in chg & b, ey inside.
128 Stylized tree, bk trunk, g foliage, spots, on child's mug.
129 Child's mug, 'Pamela' in chg.
130 Flower & bands.
131 Ship mug.
132 Banding in y, bk, chg, y & very pale y.
133–134 Not used
135 Banding in b, ey, g, wavy band g, tgo circular spots.
136 Banding, as 122, b instead of tgo, chg instead of y.
137 Floral border, in kb, tgo, o, ag & g.
138-142 Banding in russet g, v, chg. 139 gy, b, y & chg. 140 kb, sy, russet & sgy. 141 ag, v, chg & pale y. 142 as 141 but kb instead of v.
143 String bands, in chg & ag, gs alternated.
144 String bands, in v, chg, b, v, ey.
145 Floral, printed g, enamelled in y, ag, chg, rbn, ey, sgy.
146 Vertical stripes, colours as 141.
147 Vertical stripes, as 146 but kb instead of v.
148 Golden Corn, printed as wheat pattern 113.
149 Broad brush-stroke flowers, b, y & t, leaves in g.
150 Floral, kb, pale y, leaves ag, sim. to 66.
151 Tulips, simple flower kb, o, stems ag, r semi-circles.
152 Tulips, as 64, o, y tulips, ag leaf & rbn spots.
153 Floral, t, y, ey, leaves chg, bk behind stems.
154 Symphony in 3 flats, o, ey, bk flats on y glaze.
155 Spots, chg, b, irregular spots.
156 String bands, chg, kb, russet, g, y.
157 Banding, b, chg, rbn, y, on y glaze.
158 Gold lines washed in g lustre.
159-160 Lightning, lustre decoration.
161 Tulip, as 99 but shades of pink, g & gy as 64.
162 Tulip, as 152 but colouring pattern as 99.
163 Tulips, in o, kb & tgo, pale y, foliage g, ag, tgo edge.
164 Tulips, as 163 but tulip ey instead of tgo.
165 Bands, dontils & spots, in ey, b & bk.
166 Slight floral, as 150 but rbn instead of tang.
167 Banded pattern, in chg, y, tgo & bk.
168 Banding, in b with scalloped chg band & ey spots.
169 Stripes, in light b, chg, g, g edge, cruet all over in y.
170 Fruit, pink, v, b, leaves sgy, sbn, background bk.
171 Bronze chrysanthemums, as 96 on y glaze.
172 Banding, in b & chg on a wash of russet g.
173 Graduated banding, in y, tgo & bk, on a wash of thin y.
174 The Storm, t & bk lightning, clouds sgy.
175 Banding, in ag, kb, pale y, sgy.
176 Banding, as 175 but wider & touching.
177 Geometric, in b, bk, g & l.
178 Floral, as 149, o instead of tgo & edge in g.
179 Peacock feathers, in g, pale y, chg, bk.
180 Banding, as 115, v dontil edge, kb band.
181 Broken colour effects, sgy & sy.
182 Broken colour effects, sgy, kb mottled, spots bk.
183 Broken colour effects, sgy, spots g, bk, gy mottling.
184 Modernist, dontilled arcs bk, gpy, filled with gyb.
185 Banding in y, ey & rbn, with scalloped bk at base.
186 Mottled effects, gy, scrolling bk, gy, b, y, chg.
187 Mottled effects, sgy, sbn, wavy lines bk, y, sbn, gy.
188 Mottled effects, sgy, large b spots, waves bk.
189 Mottled effects, sgy, chg & bk wavy bands, spots.
190 Modernist, g bands, top zig-zag lines with v.
191 Banded & dontilled, v, b, gpy, chg & bk.
192 Banding, ey, dontils, square spots b, scallops bk, b.
193 Rhythm, gy lines filled with b, y & bk dontils.
194 Citrons, fruit y, leaves ag & chg, arcs of gy & bk.
195 Modernist, scallop bands y, chg, gy 'sharks fins'.
196 Wem shape.
197 Wem shape jugs, vases, etc.
S198 Rose & silver on a y glaze.
S199 Stylized floral in silver, banding in ag.

May 1931

S200 Stylized floral, as 199 but on y glaze.
S201 Feather pattern in silver, spots silver & gy.
S202 Silver animals, hare, squirrel & tortoise.
203 Modernist, dontilled & spiked lines, bk, b, g, l, gy.
S204 Crocus in o, y, rbn, g, ag, band in g, silver edge.
205 Slight daisy, in kb, y, g & chg.
206 Banding, in y, bk, rbn, g, bk with y band in top.
207 Floral, as 66 but on a y glaze.
208 Banding, in chg with dontils, b, dark & bright ey.
209 Banding, in y, b & chg.
210 Banding, in y, rbn, bk, inside tang, rbn, bk.
211 Banding, in tgo, gy, y, inside y, gy, tgo, bk, y.
212 Floral, gy, o, pale y, ag, lg, o & g bands at edge.
213 Floral, ey, b, gy, o, y, leaves in lg, sgy handles.
214 Floral pattern, sim. to 213.
215 Banding, in y, g, narrow bk & rbn.
216 Modernist, arcs in bk, b, sgy, g circular spots.
217 Tulips, in v, leaves ag & g, background sgy.
218 Peacock feathers, in g, pale y, chg & bk.
219 Peacock feathers, in g, b & y.
220 The Pasture, nursery ware, piglet, cow, donkey, lamb, goose, 'wee maid' with b frock.
221 Roosters, nursery ware, outlines in ag, b, pale y, ey, comb t.
222 Modernist, pointed arcs in bk, gy, semi-circles g.
223 Floral, in o & y, sbn leaves.
224 Marsh marigold, floral in y, gs.
225 Floral, sim. to 223 but b, buff o.
226 Deer leap, painted deer motif in bns.
227 Wavy bands, in chg, b, gpy, spots ey, chg strokes
228 String bands, in sgy, y, sbn, bk, hbn.
229 Banding, in y, chg dontils, b & ey narrow band.
230 Modernist, bands g, bk, g, strokes gy, bk, y spots.
231 Modernist, as 222, y, gy, g bands, y semi-circles.
232 Banding, in pale y, tgo, kb, wavy bands & lg band.
233 Spots in g, o dontilled band, b & g band.
234 Broken effects, in sgy, g, bk & chrome, bk inside.
235 Banding, o, b with dontils, chg & narrow ey band.
236 Geometric, gy lines, o, ag, y, pbn lozenge shapes.
237 Geometric, in ey, bk, o, y, pbn & hbn.
238 Feathers, feathers & foliage in bn, bk, y, o, g.
239 Symphony, as 154 but spots in tgo, chg, kb & y.
240 Crocus, as 111 but in kb, ag & g.
241 Scarlet runner beans, in rbn, bk, y & hbn.
242 Spots, g, ag, y, bands y, mixture of 239 & 241.
243 Modernist, bulbous sections, bk, y, t, arcs in gy.
244 Tadpoles, arcs & semi-circles in o, y, bk, gy, ag.
245 Banding, in y, pbn with dontils, y & ey.
SL246-SL248 Hunting scenes with lustre.
249 Not used.
250 Stylized floral, as S200, g instead of ag on y glaze.
251 Broken colour effects, washed y vase, sgy, pbn.
252 Squares & circles, overlapping, in y, bk, gy, gpy.
253 Swirling motif on 8" vase.
254 Geometric.
255 Geometric, blocks, gpy, dark bn, pbn, sbn, sgy, g.
256 California, floral, b, rbn, o, y, ag, lg, bk, on y glaze.
257 Rabbit, nursery ware, y & bn, leaping over grass.
274 Floral, sim. to 214 but t, y, dark b, y, g & sbn.
275 Not used.
276 Geometric, as 110, with g section.
277 Abstract, y, o, ag & rbn with bk sgraf section.
278 Broken banding, with sgraf.
279 Broken banding, as 273 with bk sgraf section.
280 Broken banding, as 279 but lg instead of t, gpy instead of bk.
281 Geometric, in t, gpy, y, sbn & bk, sgraf zig-zags.

Crown Works

August 1931

282 Galaxy, in b with sgraf circles, bk, gy & gpy.
283 Ovals, in lg, o, bk spot in centre, lines on hollow.
284 Bright floral, y glaze, gpy, b, t, y, sy, foliage in chg & lg.
285 Floral edge, in tgo, kb, y, ag, lg.
286 Chintz spray as diaper, in tgo, g, kb & bk.
287 Floral, as 256 but ivory, t instead of rbn, kb instead of b.
288 Geometric decoration, as 110, colours as 237.
289 Broken bands, tgo, y, gy & bk with sgraf.
290–292 Bronze chrysanthemums, sim. to 96 but b, rbn & sy flowers, leaves g & hbn. 291 leaves in g & bk, centres of flowers surrounded by bk spots. 292 as 291 but leaves in g & sgy.
293 Marigold flowers, in tang, b, sy.
294 Floral, as 274 on ivory glaze.
295 Bronze chrysanthemums, as 96 on ivory glaze.
296 Floral, in kb, leaves sgy, lg & mixed g on y glaze.
297 Abstract, maroon, gpy, y, bk & ey, on a y glaze.
298 Geometric, in hbn, old g, y, sgy, wavy bk, g.
299 Sectional banding, in gy with russet g panel.
300 Geometric, as 110 but ey & b & sbn lines.
301 Fruit, as 170 but b, y, gy & no dontils.
302 'M' monogram, shaded bands in gy.
303 Design with silver mounting, in tgo, ag, o & bk.
304 Abstract for silver mounting, gy, old g, pink, y, bk.
305 Banding, in o, rbn & bk.
306 Panorama, bk, b, bn, gy, g, jaffa, pale y, edge jaffa.
307 Campanulas, floral in kb, o, sy, lg, pale y, tgo, hbn.
308-312 Floral edge, in tgo, y, t, gy, hbn. 309 in ag, sy, rbn, y, hbn. 310 in gy, hbn, kb, y. 311 in gy, g, y, rbn, kb. 312 in g, o, y, ag, b.
313 Sectional banding, in jaffa, y & bk, bk spots.
314 Modernist, g triangles, bk squiggles, o spots.
315 Geometric, in straw y, gy, g, o, bk, spots in o on straw y section.
316 Geometric, as 315 but straw y, y, o, bk wavy sgraf.
317 Woodpecker, hbn, sgy, mixed g, y, bk & pink.
318–323 Cats with lettering, bk cats, b, g, jaffa edge. 319 gy cats, b lettering, g edge. 320 bk cats, tgo lettering & edge. 321 gy cats, tgo lettering. 322 bk cats, b lettering. 323 g lettering, g grass.
324 Acorns, incised decoration.
325 Rams, incised decoration.
326 Townscape, incised decoration.
327 Caravan, gypsy van on road in tgo, bk, y, g.
328 Freesia, floral printed & enamelled, y, o & g.
329 Caravan, gypsy van on road, rbn, jaffa edge.
330 Stylized floral, large leaves in b, chg & hbn.
331 Abstract linear, in bk, o, b & r with spots & dontils.
332 Bulbous leaf forms, in y, r, b, bk, chg finger-like leaves.
333 Floral, in b, jaffa, r, bk, mixed g, chg, gy, y.
334 Floral edge, dark g, b, bk, jaffa, gy, pbn, g, puce.
335 Floral edge, stylized leaves in jaffa, bk, g, gy, b, pbn.
336 Balloon-seller & flower-seller lamp stand.
337 Cowboy & Mexican dancer lamp stand.
338 Nosegay floral, in b, gy, sy, chg, pink.
339 Floral, in b, g, y, pink, chg, jaffa.
340 Tiger lamp stand, tiger in o & gy with bk & hbn.
341 Stylized foliage, in chg, b, r, gy, t & bk.
342 Banding, in sy, b, bk with dontils & chg.

343 Banding, in b, gpy, bk, arcs chg, o spots, bk motifs.
344 Banding, for tankards.
345 Squirrels, incised decoration.
346 Tulips, u-g, bk & b, with turq glaze.
347 Brush-stroke flowers, jaffa & pink, chg, ag leaves.
348 Briar rose, floral in pink & b, with ag leaves.
349 Stylized leaf & wavy lines in u-g bk & b, jade glaze.
350 Leaves, in bk u-g, dipped in jade g.
351 Oval spots, in bk & b u-g, dipped in jade g glaze.
352 Monkey, in hbn, bn, sgy, straw y, aub.
353 Deer, in hbn, gy, sy & gpy on aub.
354 Clown lamp base in gy, tgo, r, y, b & bk.
355 Floral lamp base.

March 1932

356 Stylized floral, in g, sgy, hbn, aub.
357 Brush-stroke flowers, in jaffa, o & hbn leaves.
358 Brush-stroke flowers, in r, g leaves.
359 Brush-stroke flowers, in r & b, bk & o centres.
360 Brush-stroke flowers, in o, b & r, clear glaze.
361 Brush-stroke flowers, in o, g & b, bk filled in.
362 Brush-stroke flower, in r, o centre & sbn leaves.
363–364 Not used.
365 Brush-stroke flowers, in pbn, y, hbn & g leaves.
366 Brush-stroke flowers, as 358 on g glaze.
367 Brush-stroke flowers, in b, r, circle & dash, clear glaze.
368 Linear, semi-circles, spots & dontils, lines bk, b, g.
369 Not used.
370 Abstract linear, in chg, g, b, tgo & jaffa.
371 Raised crocus pattern, dipped buff glaze.
372 Floral & crosses.
373 Modernist, broken banding in y, g, bk motifs, sgraf fish in bk band.
374 Floral, in r, jaffa & tgo o, chg, g, bk, bn.
375 Floral, b scalloped flowers.
376 Floral, on g glaze, broad stylized leaves, sim. to 330.
377 Stylized leaf & wavy bands, on g glaze.
378 Bands & spots, g, b with jaffa spots.
379 Bands, in y, chg, b with spots.
380 Bands, in b, jaffa, tgo, y with spots.
381 Bands, in b, hbn, jaffa, y with spots.
382 Banded, in b, bn jaffa & y.
383 Wide bands, in b, o & y.
384 Floral, sim. to E347 but r, o, y, bn dashes.
385 Floral, in u-g b & bk.
387 Black pom, dog in silhouette, b band & dontils.
388 Black pom, dog in silhouette, tgo band & dontils.
389 Floral, broad brush-stroke flowers.
390 Floral, in y, jaffa, bn, b, g & bk.
391 Floral, in g, o, maroon, b & bk.
392 Broken bands, sgraf spots, bk, glad g, y, straw y.
393 Banded, in straw y with sgraf spots in bk.
394 Stylized leaf, crosses & spots in u-g bk & b.
395 Wheat pattern in u-g b & bk.
396 Victorian sprig, floral with cross & spot edge.
397 Rodeo, cowboy printed & enamelled with cactus.
398 Rodeo, as 397, with b, tgo & jaffa bands finish.
399 Palm tree, in hbn, bn.
400 Palm tree, with mountains & lake in b & maroon.
401 Palm tree, silhouette in bk, printed u-g.
402 Floral, in u-g b & bk with jade g glaze.
403 Abstract u-g pattern, geometric & wavy scrolls.
404 Stylized floral, in u-g, tulip leaf & spot.
405 Stylized floral, in tgo, chg, bn, b & bk.
406 Red fox lamp holder with abstract floral.
407 Galleon & fish, in sbn, hbn, bn, y & gy.
408 Stylized floral, in u-g.
409 Leaping deer, as E226 but bolder, in sbn, hbn, cbn, bn & sy.
410 Banded, in g, pale y, straw y, bk & chg.
411 Deer, u-g bk, floral border, jade glaze.
412 Tulip, in u-g bk with turq jade glaze.
413 Floral, in jaffa, b, y, ag, g, hbn & bn.
414 Floral, in pastel pink, y, pbn & jaffa.
415 Banded & square dontil pattern in y, b, chg & g.
416 Banded & dontil pattern, in tgo, y, g & b.
417 Banding, spots & dontils, in y, b, jaffa & dark g.
418 Banding & spots, in y, bn, chg, g & b.
419 Banding & spots, in y, hbn, bk, tgo with tgo spots.
420 Floral spray, in u-g b & bk, jade g glaze.
421 Pheasant, u-g bk & b dash & crescent edge.
422 Pheasant & stylized foliage, in u-g bk & b.
423 Woodpecker, painted u-g.
424 U-g floral, ribbons centre to edge b & bk.
425 Stylized floral in u-g b & bk.
426 Stylized wavy leaf & floral, crescents & lines.
427 Stylized leaf, u-g b & bk, wavy lines, jade g glaze.
428 Oval leaf & wavy point in u-g.
429 Oak apple, g colouring crosses & band.
430 Oak apple, b colouring spots & band.
431 Shepherd's purse, floral in o, y, chg, ag, wavy band.
432 Blue freesia, y & pink band edge with b dontils.
433 Nosegay with g edge & dash.

September 1932

434 Shamrock entwined in ag, g band & tgo edge.
435 Floral, in pastel shades.
436 Floral, with bluebells & r flowers, jaffa, ag & gy.
437 Floral spray, in b, jaffa, tgo, chg leaves.
438 Floral spray, in pink, y, o, gy, pbn & g cross & spots.
439 Leaf, incised, vertical oval stylized leaf & triangle.
440 Leaves & flowers, incised, stylized.
441 Leaf & tulips, incised, with spots.
442 Orchids & stylized leaves, incised.
443 Scrolling stylized leaves (shrimps) incised.
444 Floral spray, in b, y, chg, r, bk, sponged o background.
445 Floral spray, as E444 with variation in floral.
446 Crocus pattern.
447 Wreath of flowers, flowers in b, jaffa tgo & y.
448 Slight crocus spray in pink, y, g, gy & jaffa.
449 Tulip spray.
450 Blue freesia, with b scallops at edge.
451 Country bunch, floral in coral b, jaffa, ag & r.
452 Canterbury bell, bluebells & zig-zag ground.
453 Flower spray, brush-stroke flowers in b, y, g.
454 Not used.
455 Chatham ashtray, in g, chg, jaffa, tgo band, cbn, bk.
456 Chatham ashtray, with the name in the design.
457 Chatham, house in landscape with trees, in g, chg, b, y.
458 Country bunch, as 451 but b scallop edge.
459 Floral, as 376 but on a primrose glaze.
460 Banded, in b, ag & jaffa with r & b spots.
461 Banded, in hbn, y, tgo, bk spots & wavy tgo line.
462 Banded, as 461 but b instead of tgo.
463 Banded, as 461 but chg instead of tgo.
464 Banded & spots, in jaffa, gpy, chg, b with bk spots.
465 Banded & spots, in hbn, pbn, gpy, y with bk spots.
466 Fishes (newts) on regina plates, ag, g sea.
467 Gladioli, as 328 in y, pink, b, g, light & dark hbn & pbn.
468 Banded with dontils, gy & g bands, chg dashes.
469 Banded & scalloped border, o spots, as 431.
470 Conventional floral, broad wavy flowers in o & y.
471 Outline floral, in b, y & tgo, with g leaves.
472 Outline floral, sbn outline, with tgo inside & y.
473 Outline floral, as 472 but turq instead of tgo.
474 Outline floral, as 472 but flower not filled in.
475 Banding & spots, hbn, pink, pink spots in bands.
476 Banding & spots, as 475, mixed gy & b, spots g.
477 Banding & spots, as 477 but variation.
478 Banding, in madder, b scallops & turq band.
479 Banding, wash-banding in gy, hbn, bn & pbn.
480 Banding, wash-banding in gy, hbn, bn.
481 Banding, wash-banding gy & g, dontils in g band.
482 Banding, wash-banding, as 481 b replacing g.
483 Banding, wash-banding, as 481 without dontils.
484 Banding, solid in hbn, bn, pbn, jaffa crosses in pbn.
485 Banding, as 484 but hbn, bn, bk, jaffa, bk crosses, y inside.
486 Banding, as 485 but b g instead of y.
487 Banding, as 485 but y g instead of y.
488 Banding, as 485 but tgo instead of y.
489 Banding, as 485 but Turkish light b instead of y.
490 Banded, in hbn, bk, y with edge of spots & crosses.
490b Banded, as 490 but dark bn replacing bk.
491 Banded, as 490 but mixed b g instead of y.
492 Banded, as 490 but jaffa instead of y.
493 Banded, as 490 but glad g instead of y.
494 Banded, as 490 but tgo instead of y.
495 Banded, as 490 but Turkish light b instead of y.
496–501 Graduated bk bands with tgo, y, jaffa o, glad g, mixed b g, light b.
502 Floral, simple centre motif, in tgo, y, hbn.
503 Conventional floral, in gy, hbn, pbn.
504 Geometric, arcs of banding, in tgo, jaffa, hbn, bk.
505 Leaf pattern, stylized leaf & flower, in ys & gs.
506 Leaf pattern, sim. to 502 but leaf in b, flower g.
507 Banding for lamp bases, in pbn, hbn, gy.
508 Banding pattern for lamps, in y, pink, hbn, gy.
509 Banding for lamps, 3 u-g pairs of g bands.
510 Banding for lamps, in y, gy, g, turq, gy & bk.
511 Banding, in tgo & hbn, bk bands finished in y & tgo.
512 Banding, in y, tgo with wavy line, gy, bk & tgo.
513 Floral (Original Florida), flowers in pink, bk & g leaves.
514 Floral, as 513 but r & tgo flowers with hatched centres.
515 Cubic, abstract with sections of bk, y, g & b.
516 Floral, in pink, tgo, y, g, bk background.
517 Geometric, as 298, with b wavy section & bk.
518 Country flowers, in o, b, y, spiked leaves in g.
519 Floral, u-g with bk aero background.
520 Stylized leaf at edge in b, hbn, bn dontils & dots.
521 Pheasant, in silver.
522 Stylized floral, in silver.
523 Aero, gyb inside cup, b outside with silver line on handle & edge.
524 Aero, as 523, g inside cup, pink outside.
525 Aero, as 523, bk inside cup, as 971 outside.
526 Aero, as 523, cela inside cup, celeste outside.
527 Aero, as 523, flame inside cup, cela outside.
528 Aero, as 523, pink inside cup, gy outside.
529 Aero, as 523, b inside cup, cela outside.
530 Aero, as 523.
531 Abstract, in t, o & bk, blocks & lines, bk spot.
532 Abstract, broken banding with letter R, sy & r.
533 Broken banding, in gy, t, as 278.
534 Banding, in wavy o & t with bk band.
535 Banding, as 534, with o shaded light to dark.
536 Banded, scalloped t band, bk spots, o, bk bands.
537 Banded, scalloped t band, bk crescents.
538 Country flowers, as 518 but bk instead of y & g.
539 Not used.
540 Outline floral, in b, tgo, y, gy, bk, chg, mixed y g.
541 Pheasant.
542 Leaf.
543 Graduated bk bands, as 496 but broader lines.
544 Pheasant, printed in b u-g, bird in peach, g.
545 Scrolls, calligraphic, in u-g mazarine b, b glaze.
546 Monogram u-g motif in bk, dipped in g glaze.
547 Leaves, in bn, y, bk, silver scalloped edge, aub.
548 Scrolls & bands, in hbn, rbn, silver, aub.
549 Pheasant, as 544 but hand-painted & silver edge.
550 Stylized floral, chg, y, bk, pbn, b, jaffa, aub.
551–553 Stylized floral, in g, y, rbn, aub.
554 Floral with cherries.
555 Floral, painted in l, b, jaffa, tang, g, bk.
556 Banded, in sy, y, hbn, gy, bk.
557 Brush-stroke floral edge, in pbn, p, y, chg leaves.
558 Broken banding, as 533, g instead of t.
559 Broken banding, as 533, Kew g instead of t.
560–561 Stylized floral, aub, on lampstand.
562 Floral, matt glaze, vases.
563 Smoke curls, carved on ashtray, buff glaze.
564 Smoke curls, carved on Limerick ashtray.
565 Floral, carved on Limerick ashtray, turq.
566 Diagonal design, carved, with flame glaze.
567 Smoke curls, carved, with b glaze.
568 Floral, carved, with y glaze.
569 Waves, carved on Donegal ashtray, b glaze.
570 Dashes, carved on base of Donegal ashtray.
571 Circles, carved on base of Donegal ashtray.
572 Floral, carved, gy jade glaze on Killarney ashtray.
573 Fruit & floral, carved on Killarney ashtray.
574 Smoke curls, on Killarney ashtray.
575 Abstract lines, on Killarney ashtray.
576 Peacock feathers, silver band.
577 Diagonal lines & spots on triangular lamp.
578 Diagonal lines, g, bn, y, on triangular lamp.
579 Diagonal lines.
580 Diagonal lines, bn, pbn, bk.
581 Playing card motifs, on hbn all over.
582 Playing card motifs, on ag, maroon motifs.
583 Playing card motifs, on madder, pbn motifs.
584 Playing card motifs, silver.
585 Playing card motifs, on sy, bk motif.
586 Playing card motifs, on turq, maroon motifs.
587 Peacock feathers, y band & g dontil band.
588 Simple floral edge.
589 Simple floral edge.
590 Spiky spot motifs, kb & ag spikes.
591 Circles, in tgo & bk.
592 Simple floral edge, in jaffa, g leaves.
593 Simple floral edge, y, o, bn, gy.
594 Aero colour inside & out.
595 Wavy sea, as E466 but without fish.
596 Wavy sea, as E466 but without fish.
597 Monogram bands & initials, with cela glaze.
598 Plaid, hbn & g.
599–603 Not used.
604–607 Round ashtrays with carved scrolls & lines.
608 Conventional floral edge.
609 Conventional floral edge.
610 Floral, in pink & p.
611 Floral, with y sponged background.
612 Goat, on honey glaze in hbn, bn, y.
613 Spots & spikes, tgo spikes as 590.
614 Stylized foliage u-g.
615 Calligraphic scrolls, in u-g b & bk, b glaze.
616 Calligraphic loops, in u-g bn & bk, gy glaze.

Spring 1933

617 Calligraphic scrolls, in g & bk, g glaze.
618 Calligraphic bk cross & bn & bk scrolls.
619 Calligraphic.
620 Calligraphic b swirls.
Little Bo-peep nursery ware (no pattern number)
621 Stag.
622 Simple floral edge, as 589 but tgo instead of g.
623 Simple floral edge, as 588 but b.
624 Banded, in pink & hbn, as 475 but no spots.
625 Banding.
626 Banding.
627 Broken banding, as 533 but tgo instead of t.
628 Bands & dontils on Wedge candlestick, in tgo, y, bk.
629 Abstract on Wedge candlestick, ovals in tgo & y, hbn lines.
630 Stylized floral on Wedge candlestick.
631 Triangles on Wedge candlestick.

632 Stripes on Wedge candlestick, in bk, b, y, g.
633-642 Banded designs on Wedge candlesticks: 633 b, gy, 634 oak apple, ag, bronze g, with spots in g, 635 hbn, oak apple, bronze g, 636 fawn, bronze g, oak apple, 637 b, lemon y, gy, y, 638 marigold, lemon y, fawn, 639 pink, fawn, oak apple, ermine tails in bk, 640 lemon y, oak apple, bronze g, 641 marigold, lemon y, hbn, 642 b, hbn, gy.
643 Stylized landscape & house ashtray, 'Royal'.
644 Stylized landscape & house ashtray, 'Imperial'.
645 Stylized landscape & house ashtray, 'Royal'.
646-648 Wash-banding, with b, hbn, ag & light b.
649 Not used.
650 Banding, with spots & crosses pbn instead of bk.
651 Gillyflower & marigolds.
652 Gillyflower & marigolds, lemon y flowers.
653 Calligraphic flourish, in bk under a terracotta glaze, pink inside.
654 Calligraphic flourish, in bk, white u-g, cela inside.
655 Calligraphic flourish, in bk, cela inside & out.
656 Banding, wash-banding with ag.
657 Pink hydrangea, in pink, b, bn crayon, bk u-g.
658 Graduated bk bands, colour on edge, tang.
659 Graduated bk bands, as 658, tang outlined bk.
660 Graduated bk bands, inside band outlined bk.
661 Graduated bk bands, as 659 but sahara pink.
662 Graduated bk bands, as 659 but pink.
663 Graduated bk bands, as 658 but pink.
664-666 Graduated bk bands, as 658–660 but ag.
667-669 Graduated bk bands, as 658–660 but light b.
670-672 Graduated bk bands, as 658–660 but y.
673-675 Graduated bk bands, as 658–660 but scarlet.
676-678 Spiral, tube-lined on mwg, terracotta, g.
679 Dropped lines, tube-lined in bk on mwg.
680 Dropped lines, tube-lined in bk on terracotta.
681 Dropped lines, tube-lined in bk on cela.
682 Not used.
683 Plaid, as 598 but b dashes & tgo circles.
684 Stylized leaves, in u-g bn, bk, y, maize glaze.
685 Stylized leaves, in u-g bn, bk, y, terracotta glaze.
686 Curls, in u-g bn crayon with shaded band.
687 Flowers & leaves, in bn, g, pink, y, crayon.
688 Convolvulus, crayon floral, b, g, bn, y, o.
689 Flowers & leaves, in bn, g, o, y, crayon.
690 Floral, tube-lined with y & flame paint, cela.
691 Convolvulus, crayon floral, y, o, g, bn.
692 Scrolls, carved, as 615.
693 Abstract, carved decoration on candlestick.
694 Floral, carved decoration on candlestick.
695 Blue iris, printed in g & painted.
696 Pink carnation.
697 Floral, tube-lined y & flame-painted terracotta.
698 Wash-banding, as 479 with deep burnt amber.
699 Wash-banding, as 479 with pink in verge.

1934

700 Banding, in bn & b.
701 Abstract, as 629 but ag instead of tgo.
702 Sprig, u-g y, bn, bk.
703 U-g in bn & bk.
704 Banding & wavy, as 535, bk, tgo, y, o, wavy scarlet.
705 Reserved for 479 variation, for Fondeville.
706 Banding & wavy, as 704 but reversed.
707 Calligraphic flourish, as 653 but b glaze.
708-719 Not used.
720 Terracotta plain glaze.
721 Terracotta, as 720, hollow ware, tube-lined bk whirl.
722-732 Tankard jug, banding top to bottom in: 722 o, bk, jade g, bk. 723 y, b, b, chg. 724 tgo, hbn, b, b. 725 y, hbn, b spots, hbn, tang. 726 o, chg, g, chg. 727 o, b, tgo, o spots. 728 y, b, ag, b, ag. 729 y, o, pbn, o, bk, o, pbn. 730 y, b spots, b, pbn, b. 731 chg, g, pbn, chg. 732 gy, y, o, pbn.
733 Floral, b, g.
734-736 Harebell: rbn flower & ag leaves, b flower &g leaves, rbn flower & bk leaves.
737 Hydrangea, as 657 but b instead of pink, finish b on-g.
738-745 Badge 'M', in various pbn, bk & bn & bands.
746 Badge 'MCS', fine-line.
747 Dontilled curl, in u-g bk & sbn.
748 Abstract, as 629, b.
749-750 Wash-banding, in: hbn & y, hbn & b.
751 Goat plaque, rbn & silver finish on honey glaze.
752 Deer plaque, rbn & silver finish on honey glaze.
753 Hound plaque, rbn & silver finish on honey glaze.
754 Tiger plaque, rbn & silver finish on honey glaze.
755 Leopard plaque, rbn & silver finish on honey glaze.
756 Graduated bk bands, as 671, water g.
757 Bands.
758 Curly bn crayon, aub.
759 Stave musical symbol, in bn & pink crayon, amethyst glaze.
760 Reserved for Fondeville.
761 Narrow bk.
762 Gillyflower, in y, pbn, g, cbn, ag.
763 Gillyflower & marigold, in pink, y, pbn, fawn.
764 Floral, in pink & b.
765 Egyptian figure, in pbn, b & chg.

766 Pyramids, in scarlet & bk.
767 Ram's head, u-g bn & pink.
768 Lotus flower, in l, b, pbn & chg.
769 Country flowers, as 518 but y instead of tgo.
770 Stylized leaves, in u-g crayon bn, b, g.
771 Seed pod, in u-g g & bn crayon.
772 Stylized flower & leaf, in u-g crayon pink, g.
773–774 Reserved.
775 Stylized leaf, in silver & pbn leaf.
776 Stylized leaf, in silver & water g leaf.
777 Reserved.
778 Stylized leaf (serpentine), in bk, g, hbn, bn.
779 Shaded bands, in g, gy, madder.
780 U-g lines, 1 bk & 1 bn, gy glaze.
781 U-g lines, 1 bk & 1 bn, cela glaze.
782 U-g lines, 1 bk & 1 bn, honey glaze.
783 Scrolls, as 545 but bn & honey glaze.
784–789 Vertical graduated bk bands & variations, with r semi-circle & lines at 90°.
790 Lines & S-shape, bk, filled with tgo.
791–795 Reserved for variations of 790.
796 Blocks of bk lines with ag.
797–800 Reserved for variations of 796.
801 Monogram, as 546 but on-g bk & b.
802 Monogram, as 546 but on-g bk & tgo.
803 String bands, as 802 but tgo & bk, on-g.
804 String bands, as 803 but ag instead of tgo.
805 String bands, in pbn, oak apple & bk.
806 String bands, in hbn, y & bk.
807 Table with flowers, printed in bk & bands.
808 Table with flowers, printed in bk & hbn bands.
809 Table with flowers, printed in bk & bands.
810 Bands & crosses, as 491, no bk & spots.
811 Calligraphic lines, in mbn, with hbn stylized pods.
812 S-shaped scroll & bands, in bns.
813 Plain oyster glaze.
814 Pink & bn crayon with oyster glaze.
815 Bands, u-g gs, cela glaze.
816 Shaded lines in gy & pbn (Verman's pattern).
817 Banding, as 637.
818 Tulip, in marigold, pbn & gs.
819 Tulip, in b & g.
820 Calligraphic flourish, in bk, mwg, pink inside.
821 Leaves, in bk, sbn on edge, graduated bands bn.
822 Stylized flower.
823 Banding, as 806, but wider bands.
824 As 803, bk & b.
825 Square plate, u-g.
826 Stylized leaf, simple g leaves, u-g.
827 Curl, tube-lined in bk with cela glaze.
828 Curl, tube-lined in bk with mwg.
829 Spots & rings, in bk & pbn on bn glaze.
830 Stylized leaves, u-g in bn, russet glaze.
831 Vertical serpentine spikes, tube-lined in bk.
832 As 831 but lines horizontal.
833 Scrolls & bands, in sbn & bk u-g.
834 Wave, tube-lined in bk, mushroom glaze.
835 Wave with spots, tube-lined bk, terracotta glaze.
836 Leaf, tube-lined & painted, mushroom glaze.
837 Graduated bands, b & hbn, mwg.
838 Vertical scrolls, in bk & sbn, mwg.
839 Vertical scrolls, in bk & apri, gy glaze.
840 Graduated lines, in bn & g crayon.
841 Crayon banding, in bn & pink.
842 Crayon banding, in dark b & g.
843 Aero pink & shaded hbn, specially for Fondeville.
844 U-g, in apri, dark bn, gy glaze.
845 U-g, in bn, bk.
846 As 839 but b instead of apri.
847 Scrolls, as 615, tube-lined in bk, painted in gy.
848 Banded, pbn, y, bk.
849 Banded, gs, y, hbn.
850 Banded, b, y, hbn.
851 Banded, pink, y, hbn.
852 Banded, y, bk, hbn.
853 Banded, hbn, pbn.
854 Banded, pbn, hbn, y.
855 Banded, y, o, bk.
856 Crayon leaves, in gy & b, u-g.
857 Dontilled double spiral banding, in bn & bk.
858 Scrolls & bands, as 833 but marigold.
859 Stylized leaf spray, as 830 but on honey glaze.
860 Stylized leaf, u-g bns.
861 Stylized leaf, u-g bns & b.
862 Stylized leaf, gs.
863 Stylized leaf, as 862 but u-g bns.
864 U-g, in g.
865 Wash-banding, as 481 reversed.
866 Stylized leaves, in u-g crayon.
867 Acorns, tube-lined in g, cela glaze.
868 Acorns, as 867 but tube-lined in white.
869 Monogram, as 546 but 2 shades of b, b glaze.

870 'MBE' crayon initials, in bn & g.
871 Stylized leaves, tube-lined with gy glaze.
872 Reserved for variation of 871.
873 Calligraphic flourish, as 820 but mushroom glaze.
874 Spiral & dashes, in u-g bk with sbn.
875 Spiral travelling down pot, in apri & bn, gy glaze.
876 Black dog, tube-lined in bk, mwg.
877 Scrolling, bn u-g.
878 Not used.
879 Tube-lined in bn, mwg.
880 Tube-lined in bk.
881–882 Reserved.
883 String bands from edge, o, tgo, bk.
884 String bands from edge, y, g, b.
885 String bands from edge, y, g, b.
886 String bands from edge, g, bk.
887 String bands from edge, bk dontils.
888 String bands from edge, bk, b, hbn, graduated lines.
889 Dontilled curl, tube-lined bn & bk.
890 String bands.
891 String bands, in bn, g.
892 String bands, in tgo, silver.
893 String bands, in tgo, cela glaze.
894 Graduated bands, as 837 but mushroom glaze.
895 Banded.
896-898 Polka dot, in: tang, ag, b.
899-904 Scroll sgraf, aero in: g, turq, y, pink, scarlet, marigold.
905-910 Circle sgraf, aero colours as 899–904.
911 Leaf, u-g in bns, bk, with mushroom glaze.
912 Crayon banding, as 842, g lines & g crayon lines.
913 Celeste glaze with b line.
914 Aero turq.
915 Aero g.
916 Aero y.
917 Aero pink.
918 Banding (Brown's new pattern).
919 Three coarse lines.

1935

S920 Flowers & leaves, silver.
S921 Leaf, silver, bk & ag.
922 Dontilled curl, tube-lined in b & bk.
923 Dontilled curl, tube-lined in r, spots sbn & bk, mwg.
924 'SVC' initials, in bn & g glaze.
925 Circle & dash, g circle, bk dash.
926 Circle & dash, tgo circle, bk dash.
927 Circle & dash, b circle, bk dash.
928 String bands, as 886 with an oyster glaze.
929 Scrolling crayon u-g.
930 Bk leaf spray litho, pink shaded & spots.
931 Scrolls, in bk, pink, bn crayon, oyster pink glaze.
932 Dontilled curl, as 889, tube-lined in r, mwg.
933 Bk leaf spray, litho, g shaded & spots.
934 Pink & gy leaf, litho, pink flourishes.
935 Pink & gy leaf, litho, g flourishes, fawn shaded.
936 Pink & gy leaf, litho, pink shaded band.
937 Crayon, b, gy, g.
938 Scrolls, crayon, mwg.
939 Spiral, crayon, mwg.
940 Spiral band down pot, in sbn, mwg.
941 Spiral, in bk with g arcs, mwg.
942 Spiral & arcs, in bn, mwg.
943 Shading, in sbn & g crayon.
944 Dontilled spiral, coil & arc, in bk with bn bands.
945 Bk spiral, bn band, g crayon, mwg.
946 Dontilled swirls, in b & bk, g crayon & sbn spiral line.
947 Spiral, u-g, aub.
948 Scrolls, sbn on aub.
949 Stylized floral, u-g bn & bk, mwg.
950 Floral & leaf, in g crayon, mwg.
951 Arcs, in bk crayon, b crayon spiral, mwg.
952 Spiral, in bn, aub.
953 Spiral, in bns under aub.
954 Two feathers, in crayon, bn spiral, mwg.
955 Scrolling in b, aub.
956 Vertical scrolls, in bk & b, mwg.
957 Leaves & scrolls, in b & bn, aub.
958 Arcs & stylized leaves, in bn & bk, aub.
959 Arcs & circles, in gs, mwg.
960 Arcs, in bk & scrolls in bn & g.
961 Scrolling curls, in bk, bn.
962 Scrolls in bk, arcs in g, mwg.
963 Short spiral, in bk & bn, mwg.
964 Bn scrolls, aub.
965 Bn leaves & scrolls, aub.
966 Scrolls, in bk, mwg.
967 Spiral & spots, in bn crayon, aub.
968 Aub.
S969 Stylized floral, as S200, lg banding.
S970 Stylized floral, as S200, rbn sgraf rim.
S971 Stylized floral, as S200, shaded gy, g.
S972 Fox.
S973 Leopard.
S974 Tiger.

S975 Hound.

976-978 Not used.

979 Bn lines & bk motif, pink glaze.

980 Three coarse lines, banded.

981 Graduated bands (9), in turq.

982 Banding, in turq & g.

983 Graduated bands (11), in b.

984 Banding, in pink.

985 Graduated bands, in b.

986 Crayon design, in pink & bn.

987 String bands, in silver & g, as 892.

988 Crayon scrolls, in bk & b.

989 Graduated bk bands, as 497 reversed, y outside.

990 Bk leaf spray, as 930, slighter bands pink & gy.

991 Bk leaf spray, as 933, slighter band.

992 Pink & gy leaf litho, as 934, slighter band.

993 Not used.

994 Nosegay litho, pale g wash finish.

995 Nosegay litho, pastel g wash finish.

996 Dropped lines, tube-lined in b, celeste glaze.

997 Nosegay, with b wash.

998 Nosegay, with y wash (later o wash 1307).

999 Nosegay, with chestnut wash.

1000 Nosegay, with b g finish.

1001 Dresden, with chestnut finish.

1002 Dresden, with glad g finish.

1003 Dresden, with M&S o finish.

1004 Dresden, with canton b finish.

1005 Dresden, with pastel pink finish.

1006 Pink shaded band, as 930, without litho.

1007 Simplified floral crayon, in bk & b, mwg.

1008 Simplified floral crayon, in bk & b, oyster glaze.

1009 Honesty border, with mwg.

1010 Stylized motif, with gy glaze.

1011 Leaping deer transfer, printed deer in bns & y.

1012 Banded, in bns.

1013 Banded, pink, cbn, fawn.

1014 Swansea centre litho.

1015 See 1330.

1016 Crayon lines, as 912, u-g.

1017 Dresden, finished with g & b.

1018 Swansea, five sprays with pink wash.

1019 Vertical wavy lines, in pink, bn, bk.

1020 Scrolls, in bn & g crayon.

1021 Loops at neck, in bn & g crayon.

1022 Crayon, in bn & bk with mwg.

1023 Polka dot, in sy.

1024 Calligraphic painted motif, aub.

1025 Peacock feathers, in b, g, bk crayon.

1026 Vertical wavy lines, in pink, bn, bk crayon.

1027 Crayon scrolling loops, in g & bn.

1028 Crayon scrolling loops, in g & bn as border.

1029 Crayon scrolling loops, in pink, bn, bk.

1030 Not used.

1031 Spiral, u-g, aub.

1032 Spiral, in u-g bns, with oyster glaze.

1033 Feathery spirals, in bn & bk crayon.

1034 Stylized leaves & spiral, mushroom glaze.

1035 Spiral & leaves, in bk under terracotta glaze.

1036 String bands, in turq & silver, as 892.

1037 Pink & gy leaf litho, narrow pink edge.

1038 Wash bands wedding ring.

1039 Wash bands, in pink, bn, hbn, fawn.

1040 Swansea spray, banded with M&S o.

1041 Tulips, in b, ag, g, rbn, y, finished with tgo spots.

1042 Tulips, in b & tgo, filled in bk.

1043–1046 Banding (cheap), in: pbn & g, buttercup & g, tang & pbn, buttercup & bk.

1047 Blue primula, litho.

1048 Not used.

1049 Gardenia, as 2298, lg.

1050 Gardenia, with y band.

1051 Simple floral litho spray.

1052 Simple floral litho spray, ag & b finish.

1053–1058 Graduated bands: wide cbn & tgo, rbn & cbn, y & cbn, b & cbn, y g & cbn, b g & cbn.

1059 Banding, ag & glad g.

1060 Simple banding.

1061 Graduated lines & crosses, rbn.

1062 Graduated lines & crosses, ag.

1063 Graduated lines & crosses, sky b.

1064 Not used.

1065 Tulips, bn & b.

1066 Band & spot border, pink with bk spots.

1067 Band & spot border, b g with bk spots.

1068 Stylized florals, in u-g bns, on hors d'oeuvres.

1069 Geometric wavy line, in u-g bn, on hors d'oeuvres.

1070 Band & spot border, as 1066, ag.

1071 Shaded band & spots, g & bk spots.

1072 Fish set, fish subjects painted u-g, g & r string bands.

1073 Fish set, fish subjects painted u-g, g & b string bands.

1074 Scrolling, in bn crayon, aub.

1076-1082 Banding patterns reversed: 483, 624, 625, 698, 699, 700, 750.

S1083 Stylized floral, as S200 with pbn band.

1085 Shaded band, in b.

1086 Geometric wavy line, as 1069, in bns as 1031.

1087 Shaded, in g as 934.

1088 Shaded, in b as 934.

1089 Banded, in pink & gy as 934.

1090 Banded, in sy, M&S o, gy.

1091 Swansea centre without small sprays.

1092 Swansea centre, marigold shaded band.

1093 Marigold shaded band.

1094 Bk leaf spray, as 933, pink shaded.

1095 Bk leaf spray, as 933, M&S o shaded.

1096 Bk leaf spray, as 933, canton b shaded.

1097-1099 Brush-strokes & dashes: rbn, y, ag.

1100-1104 Brush-stroke over 2 fine bk lines in: tang, lg, b, marigold.

1105 Not used.

1106 Graduated bands, as 837, mushroom glaze.

1107 Leaping deer, in bns, aub.

1108 Fox, freehand, in bn & apri, aub.

1109 Banded, in v, p, l & bk.

1110 Banded, in p, l & bk.

1111 Banded, as 698 reversed.

1112 Banded, as 479 reversed, see 705.

1113 Graduated lines (5), in r, u-g aub.

1114 Wash bands, as 624, turq instead of pink.

1115 Wash bands, as 624, madder instead of bn.

1116 Wash bands, hbn & rbn.

1117 Wash bands, scarlet & hbn.

1118 Wash bands, mixed gy & scarlet.

1119 Wash bands, as 624, shaded madder on rim.

1120 Wash bands, as 624, turq & madder rim.

1936

1121 Stripes, bk & o, on edge hors d'oeuvres.

1122 Stripes, g & bk, on edge hors d'oeuvres.

1123 Stripes, tgo & bk, on edge hors d'oeuvres.

1124 Wavy border.

1125 Wavy border & spots.

1126 Wavy border & tgo spots.

1127 Not used.

1128 String bands, as 892, b & silver.

1129 Sgraf (Corinthian), in g, cbn band.

1130 Sgraf (Corinthian), in b, bk band.

1131 Sgraf (Corinthian), in tgo, bk band.

1132 Sgraf (Corinthian), in cbn, bk band.

1133 Sgraf (Corinthian), in canton b, cbn band.

1134 Lines & spots, turq lines, y spots.

1135 Lines & spots, rose lines, b spots.

1136 Lines & spots, turq lines, tgo spots.

1137 Lines & spots, rose lines, g spots.

1138 Banded, as 1135.

1139 Lines & spots, tgo & hbn.

1140 Dresden, g & pink string bands.

1141 Dresden, 5 sprays on rim, g finish.

1142 Dresden, shaded centre & 5 sprays.

1143 Bn & apri lines on edges, u-g, aub.

1144 Spots in turq & bk, silver-traced handles.

1145 U-g bn & bk.

1146 Nosegay, with verge lines.

1147 Crayon loop, g & b.

1148 Crayon loop, bn & b.

1149 Laurel border, sgraf, in g with cbn band.

1150 Laurel border, sgraf, cbn & g.

1151 Laurel border, sgraf, canton b & cbn.

1152 S-shaped dontilled scrolls, sgraf, in bk.

1153 S-shaped dontilled scrolls, in bk, cbn band.

1154 S-shaped dontilled scrolls, sgraf, in canton b.

1155 Feather, in g with 6 bands.

1156 Feather, in pink with 6 bands.

1157 Fern leaf, in b, see 1216.

1158 Fern leaf, in mauve.

1159 Dresden, as 1142 but 3 shaded lines.

1160 Dresden, as 1159.

1161 Pink & gy leaf, as 936, water g shaded.

1162 Pink & gy leaf, as 936, M&S o shaded.

1163 Nosegay, with cbn shaded band.

1164 Fern leaf, in pbn, g circles.

1165 Band & spot border, as 1006, cbn with bk spots.

1166 Band & spot border, canton b with bk spots.

1167 Silver vine & key border.

1168 Slight pink band, as 991, no litho.

1169 Leaf litho, in g, no finish.

1170 Nosegay, no finish.

1171 Dresden, no finish.

1172 Pink & gy leaf, pink shade, litho.

1173 Pink & gy leaf, with finish as 934.

1174 'LS' initials on rim & several fine lines, Harrods.

1175 'LS' initials on rim in bn & pink lustre, Harrods.

1176 Sgraf (Corinthian), as 1129, g, bk band.

1177 Band & spot border, turq with bk spots.

1178 Leaping deer, with g band.

1179 Wash-banding, as 624 but canton b.

1180 Aero b.

1181 Calligraphic motif, with glost glaze.

1182 Pink & gy leaf design, in crayon, spiral painted, mwg.

1183 Feather border, in bn & g.

1184–1187 Diamonds, sgraf in aero: b, t, May g, lime.

1188–1190 Exclamation mark, in: ag, b & tgo.

1191–1196 Crayon loop, in: g & pink, g & g, o & g, pink & g, y & g, bk & g.

1197–1199 Chevrons in bk, bands & lines in: g, r, bn.

1200 Wash-banding, as 1179 reversed.

1201 Laurel border, as 1151, canton b fine line.

1202 Laurel border, as 1151.

1203 Laurel border, as 1151, cbn.

1204 Not used.

1205 Swansea centre with pink shade.

1206-1208 Cheshire bands, in: b & sky b, ag & g, tgo & y.

1209 Laurel border, as 1149.

1210 Laurel border, as 1149, cbn.

1211 Laurel border, as 1149, canton b.

1212 Band & spot border, g with scarlet spots.

1213 Band & spot border, pink with g spots.

1214 String bands, in b & silver, as 892.

1215 Swansea.

1216 Fern leaf & spots, in tgo.

1217 Hand-painted lamp base.

1218 Hand-painted lamp base, rose pink.

1219 Graduated bands on lamp base.

1220 Graduated bands on lamp base, in tgo.

1221 Key border motif, in silver.

1222 Pink & gy leaf, pink shaded.

1223 Pink & gy leaf, b shaded.

1224 Pink & gy leaf, lemon shaded, honey glaze.

1225-1231 Nursery subjects: horse & jockey, Noah's ark, cowboy, bk pom & terrier, dignity & impudence, golfer, skier.

1232 Scroll border, crayon in bn & gy.

1233 Silver laurel.

1234 Leaf spray, in bk with b finish.

1235 Circles, tube-lined, with mushroom glaze.

1236 Circles & motif, motif chg, circle rbn.

1237 Circles & motif, motif g, circle rbn.

1238-1243 Crescents, sgraf in: turq, May g, ag, b, lemon, tgo.

1244 Loops, tube-lined in bk with bn paint.

1245 Loops, tube-lined in bk with bn paint, aub.

1246 Loops, tube-lined in bk with bn crayon.

1247-1250 Nursery wares: doll, antelope, elephants, giraffe, printed & enamelled.

1251 Dresden, sky b shaded, for Fondeville.

1252 Crescents, sgraf in aero pink.

1253 Reserved.

1254 Pink & gy leaf & bands, as 1090.

1255-1256 Wash-banding, as 698 & 479 reversed, with silver finish, for Fondeville.

1257 Fawn & gy crayon, as Miss C. at BIF (*sic*).

1258 Brush-stroke border, in M&S o.

1259-1263 Banding with brush-stroke border, in: g, mauve, b, M&S o, old g.

1264 Star & festoon, sgraf in pink.

1265 Floral litho on new classic shape cheap seconds.

1266 Circle & dash, in rbn.

1267 Not used.

1268-1274 Circle & chevron, sgraf in: celeste, ag, May g, mango, y, pink, Turkish b.

1275 Not used.

1276 Swansea, with cbn shaded band.

1277 Dresden, with b shaded band.

1278 Nosegay, with b shaded band.

1279 Dresden, with y shaded band.

1280 Nosegay, with y shaded band.

1281 Fish sets.

1282-1284 Cactus, with finish in: rbn & russet g, rbn & cbn, b & cbn.

1285 April floral print, in g.

1286 April floral print, in rbn.

1287–1290 Border print with on-g, in: canton b, bn, g, rbn.

1291 Printemps & Swansea border.

1292 Printemps & g Swansea border.

1293 Printemps & pink Swansea border.

1294 Swansea centre with gold line.

1295 Dresden with gold line.

1296 Laurel border in gold, as 1233.

1297 Pink & gy leaf, as 992 but canton b.

1298 Printemps in pink & animal centres.

1299 Printemps in bn & nursery.

1300 Pink shading & bk line to edge.

1301 Banding, as 833 but b.

1302-1306 Flower logs, crescent & straight, in u-g: b g, b g & old g, straight in b g.

1307-1309 Deer table centre, fox & hound, gy, mauve, bn.

1310-1312 Deer, fox & hound, to match 698.

1313a Hound, to match 479.

1313 Deer, to match 479.

1314 Fox, to match 479.

1315-1318 April, u-g print border in: b, pink, bn, g.

1319 Printemps, b border.

1320 Lines, in g, on hors d'oeuvres.

1321-1325 Not used.
1326 Moustache cup, 7 subjects.
1327 Pink & gy leaf, cbn band.
1328 Shaded band, in water g.
1329 Pink & gy leaf, as 934, b g shaded band.
1330 Swansea, with canton b shaded band.
1331 Calligraphic flourish, as 820 but bn, with aub.
1332 Bk leaf spray, as 933 with cbn wash band.
1333 Bn & gy crayon design, aub.
1334 Nosegay, with sky b band.
1335 Shaded band, in water g.
1336 Oval, sgraf in aero tang.

I December 1936

1337-1339 Wide bands with spots: pbn band with pbn spots on cbn, pbn band with pbn spots on g, pbn, b band with r spots on pink.
1340-1342 Banded in gy with spots & 5 graduated lines, in: b, g, tang.
1343 Game set, animal subjects, deer, grouse, pheasant, hare, cock.
1344 Wild ducks, two ducks motif.

1937

1345 Crayon banding, as 912, r band & bn crayon.
1346 Band & sgraf chevrons & loops.
1347 Bud, hand-painted in lg, y finish.
1348 Shamrock motif diaper, in lg.
1349 Circles & crosses, alternating, in chg & bn.
1350 April, as 1285, canton b shaded band.
1351 April, as 1285, b g shaded band.
1352 Dignity & impudence & black poms on lamp.
1353 Horse & jockey lamp, with painted landscape.
1354 Black leaf spray with pink shade, for Fondeville.
1355 Cactus, r slight finish.
1356 April, b, see 1285.
1357 Wash bands, as 479 but with pbn, for Fondeville.
1358 Crescent, sgraf in b g.
1359-1363 Circles, sgraf in aero: b, turq, May g, tgo, ag.
1364 Scrolling, in g & sbn with aub.
1365 Stylized leaf & scrolls.
1366 Stylized leaf & spots.
1367 Graduated lines (7), in b, with wavy bn crayon.
1368 Not used.
1369 Crayon banding, in g, with r bands.
1370 Crayon banding, in b with marigold bands.
1371 Crayon banding, in b with maroon.
1372 Scrolling border & sgraf circles in cbn band.
1373 Scrolling border & sgraf circles in sev band.
1374 Band of sgraf ovals, in cbn with gold line.
1375 Band of sgraf ovals, in g with gold line.
1376 Bands & spots, in tgo, g & gy shading.
1377 Bands & spots, in turq, g & gy shading.
1378 Shaded band, in g with gy.
1379-1380 Not used.
1381 Graduated lines, in tgo.
1382 Leaping deer, with cbn lines.
1383 Crayon banding, as 912, crayon u-g.
1384 Not used.
1385 Printed motif, centre in gy with cbn band.
1386 Wash-banding, as 479, for Eaton & Co.
1387 Crescents, sgraf in l, as 1238.
1388 Florence floral litho, in b.
1389 Graduated scalloped lines in y & g, on lamp.
1390-1393 Graduated bk bands, in: t & pbn, cbn, r, russet g.
1394 Not used.
1395 Canton b wash, with u-g pink & print.
1396 Ovals, sgraf in b lamp base.
1397 Commas, new cheap pattern in cbn, for Maple.
1398 Acorn, new litho, gy & g bands.
1399 Acorn, litho, with coral pink.
1400a-1400c Portcullis, in pinks & fawn.
1401 Shaded band hbn, bn dashes & spots.
1402 Shaded band M&S o, bn dashes & spots.
1403 No. 1 litho centre, bn shaded band & g band.
1404 No. 1 litho centre, g shaded band & bn band.
1405 Shaded band M&S o, cbn dashes & spots.
1406 Ribbon border, sgraf in turq, canton b band.
1407 Ribbon border with leaves & motifs sim. to 1406.
1408 Wash-banding, in b.
1409 Ribbon border, sgraf in cbn.
1410-1412 Bands, in: y & cbn, pink & cbn, pale b & dark b.
1413 No. 2 litho, canton b scallop border.
1414 Wash-banding, in b & g.
1415 Scrolls & chevrons, sgraf in bk band.
1416 Nursery subject lithos: cockerel & hens with clouds, 550 house, pig & cow, 551 duck up hillside, 552 sailing boat & anchor, 553 cow, sheep, cockerel & pig, 554 Jack in the box & trumpet, 555 train, 556 marching soldiers.

1938

1417 Endon border.
1418 April, u-g pink border.
1419 Stylized leaf, u-g crayon, as 912 with 6 b lines.
1420-1425 Flower, spots & scallop edge, in: pink, b, y, g, tgo, turq with b spots & scallop.
1426 Wash-banding, as 1410.
1427 Not used.
1428 Wide band, in gy, pbn band.

1429-1430 Not used.
1431 Crescents, sgraf on turq border and pink line.
1432 Bands & dontils, as 648 reversed.
1433 Wash-banding, as 698 reversed, for Fondeville.
1434 Wash-banding, as 479 on lamps, for Fondeville.
1435 Scroll pattern, in cbn.
1436 Nursery, horse, goose, lamb, pig, ship.
1437 Wash-banding, as 699 reversed.
1438 Wash-banding, as 479 but M&S o instead of pbn.
1439 Wash-banding, as 479 but tgo instead of pbn.
1440 Swansea centre, cbn wash.
1441-1446 Aub with solid aero inside, in: pink, r, y, b, turq, g.
1447 Fern in g crayon as border, with lime matt glaze.
1448 Fern in bn crayon, under aub.
1449 Wavy border in g, matt lime glaze.
1450 Wavy border in bn, aub.
1451 Wavy border in g & pink, lime mwg.
1452 Wavy line & dash in p crayon, mwg.
1453-1456 Band & crosses in: bn, b, M&S o, g.
1457 Crayon, g, in ridges of Spiral shape.
1458 Crayon, p, in ridges of Spiral shape.
1459 Hors d'oeuvres, various subjects, sbn & g edge.
1460 Hors d'oeuvres, various subjects, apri 7 b edge.
1461 Chevrons & loops, sgraf, as 1346, b & gold, on Falcon.
1462 Ribbon border, sgraf, as 1406, mbn, on Falcon.
1463 Ribbon border, sgraf, as 1406, b, on Falcon.
1464-1469 Regency feather, sgraf, aero in: pink, turq, dark b, bk, chin b, sage.
1470-1473 Elderberry, sgraf, aero in: pink, turq, dark b.
1474-1475 Not used.
1476-1481 Hearts & spots on line, sgraf, aero in: pink, turq, dark b, marigold, g.
1482-1486 Leaf & spots, sgraf in aero: pink, mbn, turq, g, dark b.
1487-1491 Dashes in waves, sgraf in: turq, pink, chin b, sage, mbn.
1492 Regency feather, as 1464 but mbn.
1493 Bands & spots, as 1340, in cbn, wide M&S o bands.
1494 Bands & spots, as 1340, in pbn.
1495 Bands & spots, as 1340, in tgo.
1496 Banded bn with sgraf crosses, y wide band, bn crosses.
1497 Banded b with sgraf crosses, y wide band b crosses.
1498 Banded ag with sgraf crosses, y wide band, ag crosses.
1499 Banding in M&S o, mbn square dontils & spots.
1500 Sepia border & sprays.
1501 Leaf motif border, in chin b.
1502 As 1415, without gold.
1503 Wash banding, as 1410, b & rbn.
1504 Parrot print.
1505 Parrot print, multi-enamelled.
1506 Traditional litho, by Thos Hulme.
1507 Shaded, as 1414, dontil & spots.
1508 Shaded, as 1414, cbn & y.
1509 Not used.
1510 Scallop edge, in pbn.
1511-1515 Scallop edge, in: b, bn, sy, tgo, ag.
1516 Not used.
1517 Acorn centre, y band.
1518 Acorn centre, pbn band.
1519 Banding in M&S o, b square dontils & spots.
1520 Banding in M&S o, tang square dontils & spots.
1521-1523 Band & sgraf in: pbn, g, b.
1524-1527 Band with bn crosses, band in: y, b, g, y.
1528-1533 Band with crosses: b cross on y, b cross on M&S o, lg cross on M&S o, g cross on hbn, bk cross on y, tgo cross on M&S o.
1534-1537 Fern, sgraf in aero: b, pink, g, mbn.
1538 Not used.
1539 Litho no. 2, with g shaded band.
1540 Stylized leaf, painted in bn, mwg.
1541 Chevrons & loops, sgraf, in mbn, as 1346.
1542 Crescents, as 1238, marigold.
1543 Crescents, as 1238, mbn.
1544 Printemps.
1545-1547 Crayon in ridges of Spiral shape, as 1457, in: g, p, peacock b.
1548-1549 Spiral shape.
1550 Gold edge & tracing, on Spiral.
1551-1553 Imperial Airways symbol in b, sgraf, several sgraf symbols.
1554 Mahogany aero & gold line.
1555 Mahogany aero, g finish, on Spiral.
1556 No. 2 centre, as 1356, 2 g lines, on Spiral.
1557 Sepia rose, on Spiral.
1558 Sepia rose, with mbn border, on Spiral.
1559 Rose centre (Patricia rose), on Spiral.
1560-1561 Spiral shape.
1562 Starbursts, g & rose, on lamp.
1563 Starbursts, chin b & pink, on lamp.
1564 Leaf spot & dash, sgraf in pbn.
1565 Spiral with chin b.
1566 Peacock feathers & chevrons, in b, on lamp.
1567 Woodlands litho, on Spiral.
1568 Pineapple sgraf, in pink aero.
1569-1571 Starbursts g & rose, b & pink, chg & pink.
1572-1573 Aero in: mbn, pink, on Spiral.
1574 Endon, on Kestrel.

1575-1580 Aero covers & insides in: b, pink, cant, mbn, sev, maize, on Falcon.
1581-1582 Dresden.
1583 Cancelled.
1584-1586 Swansea & sprays, in: cela, apri, s pink.
1587 Band & sgraf, as 1521 reversed or revised.
1588 Band & sgraf, as 1522 reversed or revised.
1589 Band & sgraf, as 1523 reversed or revised.
1590 Pineapple sgraf, as 1568 turq.
1591-1596 Chevrons, lines & scallops, sgraf in: cbn, bk, pink, sage, mbn, turq.
1597 Not used.
1598 Rooster.
1599 Hen.
1600 Swan.
1601 Anemone.
1602 Vine leaf & grapes on spiral.
1603 Wash-banding, as 1179 reversed.
1604-1609 Pear, plum & grapes, sgraf in aero: bk, sage, chin b, pink, mbn, turq.
1610–1615 Pear & apple, sgraf in aero: bk, sage, chin b, pink, mbn, turq.
1616–1621 Apples, sgraf in aero: bk, sage, chin b, pink, mbn, turq.
1622-1627 Pear & cherries, sgraf in aero: bk, sage, chin b, pink, mbn, turq.
1628-1632 Grapevine, as 1602, sgraf in aero: sage, chin b, pink, mbn, turq, on Spiral.
1633 Pear & cherries, painted u-g g line, on Spiral.
1634 Pear & plum, painted u-g.
1635 Grapevine, painted u-g b line.

1939

1636 Convolvulus, litho, on Rex.
1637 Long leaf, litho, scalloped in g.
1638 Long leaf, litho, ag line & wide pink band, on Kestrel.
1639-1642 Circle & dontil edge in bn on aero: y, cela, apri, peach.
1643 Coraline, litho border, on Falcon.
1644-1646 Banding, wide & narrow, in: salmon & sy, sage & pink, mbn & sage.
1647-1649 Scallop & curl border, sgraf in aero: sage, mbn, chin b.
1650-1651 Banding, in: sage & hbn, chin b.
1652 Litho no. 2 centre, border aero in g with sgraf circles.
1653 Lines & dashes, sage lines, rbn dashes.
1654 Lines & dashes, ag lines, mbn dashes.
1655 Chinese feather, painted motif in rbn, on Falcon.
1656 Chinese feather, painted motif in sage.
1657 Patricia rose, litho with pink wash band.
1658 Patricia rose, litho with g band.
1659 Sea anemone, litho with g wash.
1660 Sea anemone, litho with pink wash.
1661 Shamrock, slight floral.
1662 Shamrock, chg & sky b.
1663 Scrolls, sgraf in aero sage.
1664 Scrolled feather, in u-g bn with dontils.
1665 Scrolled feather, in u-g French g, dashes & dontils maroon.
1666 Upright feather, maroon u-g.
1667 Scrolled feather.
1668 Scrolled feather, in fern & bn, with aub.
1669-1672 Squares diaper, print & on-g in: sy print & g, bn print & sage, bn print & cbn, pink print & sage.
1673 Scrolls, as 1663, sgraf in mbn.
1674-1677 Aero & gold line in: sage, chin b, pink, sbn.
1678 Grapevine, sgraf, as 1629, in chin b.
1679 Leaf & spots, sgraf, as 1482, in chin b.
1680 Stars printed in g, solid g inside, 1680a sage inside.
1681 Stars printed in rbn.
1682 Stars printed in pink, 1682b pink foot.
1683 Stars printed in b.
1684-1689 Stars printed in: mbn, g, rbn, pink, chin b, mbn, finished in gold.
1690-1693 Panel border litho in: b, hbn, pink, g.
1694 Scrolls with dontils in u-g bk, tgo inside.
1695 Leaf & spots, sgraf, as 1482 but sage.
1696 Ribbon border, as 1431 without crescents.
1697-1700 Pineapple, sgraf, as 1568 but aero in: bk, sage, chin b, mbn.
1701 Elegance (Eatons coffee sets) cbn print, pbn finish.
1702 Elegance cord & ring in cbn print, cbn finish.
1703 Elegance cord & ring in bk print, b finish.
1704-1705 Elegance cord & ring in cbn, finish in: g, b.
1706-1709 Elegance cord & ring in bk, finish in: pink, M&S o, glad g, tang.
1710 Elegance cord & ring in cbn, finish in tang.
1711 Stars, print in sage g, finish in gold.
1712-1714 Elegance cord & ring, border print on nesting cup in: pink, sage, chin b.
1715-1720 Aero solid colour as 1575.
1721 Convolvulus, ag brush border.
1722 Swansea, spiral circles, ag border.
1723 Swansea, spiral circles, turq border.
1724 Convolvulus, litho.
1725 Long leaf, litho pink, g, gy.
1726 Panel spray, litho.
1727 Red dog, litho, on Spiral.
1728 Black dog, litho, on Spiral.

1729 Long leaf, as 1638 with sage band.
1730 Apples, in u-g old g, fern border.
1731 Pear, apple, cherry, on Spiral.
1732 Panel spray, litho.
1733 Convolvulus, g line & wash band.
1734 Stylized leaf, in g & b.
1735 Scrolls with hatched lines, in mazarine b u-g.
1736 Stylized leaf with spots, gyb glaze.
1737 Stylized leaf, u-g print mazarine b & bn.
1738 Centre spray, painted in u-g fern & b glaze.
1739 Stylized leaf, border in u-g b & fern.
1740 Patricia rose, with b shaded band.
1741 Patricia rose, with pink star background.
1742 Mirror plate, turq aero, white dots.
1743-1744 Not used.
1745 Mirror plate, pink aero, sgraf rose & rings.
1746 Long leaf, litho, pink band with b narrow band.
1747 Long leaf, litho, ag narrow band, wide y band.
1748 Long leaf, litho, ag narrow band, pink spots.
1749 Anemone litho centre.
1750 Pink, bn border.
1751 Apple & leaves, simple painted u-g.
1752 Pink & gy leaf, as 1161 but on Spiral.
1753 Cactus, with g wash, on Spiral.
1754 Dresden, with b shaded band, on Spiral.
1755 Pink & gy leaf litho, shaded M&S o.
1756 Stars in sage with no. 1 litho centre.
1757 Stars in b litho & border.
1758 Swansea & pink circles, on Spiral.
1759-1764 Cocktail tray, 20 sgraf spots around well in: mbn, b, sage, turq, bk, pink.
1765-1770 Cocktail tray, cockerel sgraf in: sage, b, turq, pink, mbn, bk.
1771-1776 Cocktail tray, simple cockerel & egg, sgraf in: turq, pink, chin b, sage, mbn, bk.
1777-1782 Cocktail tray, circles sgraf across surface in: b, sage, mbn, bk, turq, pink.
1783-1788 Cocktail tray, cocktail glass sgraf in: pink, turq, chin b, sage, mbn, bk.
1789 Floral print & enamel, sage & b.
1790 Beechwood, hand-painted in pink, g, old g.
1791 Beechwood, hand-painted in maroon, g, old g.
1792 Stylized leaf border in u-g gs.
1793 Cockerel motif, fern, old g, rbn.
1794 Banding, u-g in maroon, old g, smoke.
1795-1797 Banding, u-g in: b, dk g, light g.
1798 Long leaf, litho, wide chin b band.
1799-1801 Star print, nesting cups, in: pink, b, sage.
1802 Lamp, freehand u-g pink & gold.
1803 Lamp, freehand fern & maroon u-g.
1804 Lamp, u-g old g, maroon.
1805 Lamp, u-g.
1806 Lamp, u-g b & cherry.
1807 Animal subjects, service plates, scroll sgraf.
1808 Animal subjects, service plates, V sgraf.
1809 Lamp, pink, simple sgraf border, 1809a no sgraf.
1810 Lamp, turq, simple sgraf border, 1810a no sgraf.
1811 Lamp, apri, simple sgraf border, 1811a no sgraf.
1812 Lamp, sbn, sgraf border, 1812a cela no sgraf.
1813-1815 Floral centre, freehand, in: sage, pink, b.
1816 Aero, in b, on Spiral.
1817-1820 Star print & aero in: pink, apri, sage, b.
1821-1823 Convolvulus, litho, bands in: b & pink, pink & sage, g & pink.

1940
1824 Rope border, in u-g b & cherry.
1825 Rope border, in u-g maroon & old g.
1826 Stylized leaves, in u-g g & bn.
1827 Stylized leaves & fern leaf, in u-g g & bn.
1828 Scrolls & stars, u-g in g, bn, old g stars.
1829-1830 Loop print, in: pink, g.
1831 Chinese feather, as 1655 but b.
1832 Motif in rbn, lines & spots in sage.
1833 Motif, lines & spots in sage.
1834 Leaf motif in rbn, between b lines.
1835 Leaf motif in b, between b lines.
1836 Blue lines with rbn hatched wavy vertical line.
1837 Stylized leaf, as 1734 in pink, g, old g.
1838 Turkey sets, painted in sbn.
1839 Convolvulus, litho with y band.
1840 Loops & circles, sgraf in pink with gold line.
1840a Sea anemone, as 1660, b wash.
1841 Woodlands.
1842-1843 Spots, in: b & red, rbn & g. Samples for Pochin, Leicester.
1844-1845 Patricia rose, aero covers in: pink, turq.
1846-1847 Dresden spray, with aero turq & pink.
1848 Banding, wide b, narrow pink.
1849-1851 Banded, simple lines, in: turq, pink, light g.
1852 Bk leaves, coffee sets.
1853 Rope border, u-g in g & bn.
1854 Fruit print in sbn, hand-painted, finish old g, g (4 designs per doz.)
1855 Fruit print, as 1854, finish in old g & maroon.
1856 Rope border, sgraf, u-g to match 1853.

1857 Rope border, sgraf, u-g bn to match 1825 & 1862.
1858 Rope border, sgraf, u-g b to match 1824.
1859 Design to match Beechwood, in bn.
1860 Design to match 1827, in g aero.
1861 Rope border, as 1825 in old g & bn.
1863-1864 Floral litho border, no finish, on: Spiral, plain.
1865-1867 Banded, as 1849, in: mauve, y, b, on Spiral.
1868-1869 Stars, in: pink as 1682, b.
1870 Fruit centre plates, print & paint u-g, band on glaze, 4 designs per dozen, 1 peach & grape, 2 apple & blackberry, 3 y plums, 4 pear & plums.
1871 Rose, painted in bn on cela u-g, as 1559.
1872 Rose, painted in pink on cela u-g, as 1559.
1873-1875 Patricia rose, sgraf in: cela, pink, s pink.
1876-1877 Dresden spray, sgraf in: pink, shade.
1878 Tulips, sgraf in g to match Endon 1417.
1879 Stylized leaf, as 1734, sgraf in cela.
1880-1883 Floral litho border, as 1863, on Spiral & plain.
1884 Not used.
1885 Floral litho border A & B.
1886-1889 Fruit centre, at 1870, with: pink, y band.
1890-1891 Patricia rose, line cela, aero g, g & old g.
1892-1895 Patricia rose, wide band & line in: b & bn, pink & sage, sage & pink, y & oak apple.
1896-1899 Dresden spray, wide band & line in: b & bn, pink & sage, sage & pink, y & oak apple.
1900-1902 Woodlands, 1901 oak apple, 1902 ag, bands.
1903 Patricia rose, wide band pink, narrow 10” sage .
1904 Patricia rose, wide band b, narrow 10” cbn.
1905 Border to match stylized leaf 1734, u-g.
1906 Border to match beechwood, u-g.
1907-1908 Patricia rose, with line in: turq, pink, on Spiral.
1909-1911 Tulip & daisy spray, finish in: pink, b, sage.
1912 Pink aster spray, on Rex.
1913-1914 Reserved.
1915 Plaque, on-g aero in u-g cela, leaf border in bn & g.
1916 Plaque floral centre sgraf in aero cela.
1917-1923 Star print, half-handles & narrow band in: b & b, pink & pink, g & pink, g & sage, b & y, pink & g, pink & b.
1924 Tiger lily litho, fern trim.
1925 Green leaf litho, line cela, aero g.
1926 Green leaf, as 933, finish glad g.
1927 Two feathers, as 935, b finish on Falcon.
1928 Bk leaf spray, as 930, pink finish, on Falcon.
1929 Pink & gy leaf, as 934, pink finish, on Falcon.
1930 Turq aero & line, on Spiral.
1931 Stylized foliage lamp base, with u-g b & g.
1932 Stylized foliage lamp base, (C16) u-g maroon.
1933 Patricia rose, ag line & wide pink.
1934 Tiger lily, small leaf edge, on Spiral.
1935-1937 Vine leaf & scroll border u-g: cela, coral, wine; 1935-1946 on plaques.
1938-1940 Pineapple, sgraf, u-g colours as 1935–1937.
1941-1943 Rose, sgraf, u-g colours as 1935–1937.
1944-1946 Tulip, sgraf, u-g colours as 1935–1937.
1947 Patricia rose, as 1894 but cela.
1948 Bands & spots, pbn line & g spots, 1948a sage line & pbn spots.
1949 Bands & spots, sage line & pink spots.

1941
1950 Patricia rose, b wavy litho border.
1951 Convolvulus, litho bands ag & gy.
1952 Pink aster spray, finish pink & M&S o, on Falcon.
1953-1954 Cornflower, finish: pink & b, pink & sage.
1955 Tiger lily, finish sage & s pink.
1956-1957 Bands & spots, pbn & sage, s pink & b.
1958-1959 Starburst, in: mbn & g, chin b & pink.
1960-1962 Pink & gy leaf, 2 narrow bands in: pink & M&S o, pink & g, g & gy.
1963-1965 Bk leaf spray, g bands, in: ag & dark g, pink & g, ag & gy.
1966 Starburst, in g & pink.
1967-1969 Bud & ring, flower & band, in: pbn & sage, sage & pink, chin b & pink.
1970-1971 Bk leaf, freehand: sage band, chin b band.
1972 Pink & gy leaf, as 934, bands in gy & g.
1973-1974 Flower motif, sage, inside: mbn, pink.
1975 Flower motif, b, pink inside.
1976-1978 Patricia rose, with aero in: pink, g, b.
1979 Band & aero, pbn aero, bands sage g & pbn.
1980 Band & aero, pink aero, bands pbn.
1981-1991 Tiger lily, as 1892, bands in: russet & madder, cbn & russet, sage & pink, pink & M&S o, sage & b, sage & kb, cbn & oak apple, pink & cbn, sage & pbn, hbn & pink with fern litho border, pink & fern border.
1992-1993 Vine centre, sgraf in aero: mbn, pink.
1994-1995 Tulip centre, sgraf in aero: pink, mbn.
1996 Aero & banded, in lemon & y.
1997 Aero covers, as 1575 in glad g.
1998 Aero covers, as 1575 in chin b.
1999 Tiger lily, as 1934, plain shape.
2000-2001 Tiger lily, shaded band in: sage, mbn.
2002 Patricia rose, russet & narrow sage bands.
2003 Magnolia, g leaf border with sepia centre.
2004 Green slip painted u-g (for litho).

2005 Tooth border, in old g & bn (for u-g litho).
2006 Orchid, painted g slip & maroon & bn.
2007 Rose, painted in g slip.
2008 Seaweed centre, sgraf & painted.
2009 Magnolia, gardenia, azalea, clematis, on Spiral plates.
2010 Clematis, with wide sage band.
2011 Dessert plates to match 2010.
2012 Azalea, Spiral dessert plates.
2013-2014 Aero in: mbn, turq.
2015 Not used.
2016-2018 Patricia rose, band & aero in: pink, turq, apri.
2019 Dresden spray, apri aero, sgraf crescents.
2020 Tiger lily, gy band & g line.

1946
2021 Starburst, with pbn aero inside.
2022 Starburst, sage & pink, aero sage.
2023 Starburst, aero y.
2024 Chinese feather in pbn, pbn aero inside.
2025 Chinese feather in sage, cela aero inside.
2026 Starburst, b & pink, b aero inside.
2027 Starburst, b & pink.
2028-2030 Bud, painted in: sage with pink aero inside, b with pink inside, b with sb inside.
2031 Little bird, in chin b, with apri aero inside.
2032 Scroll border, in bronze lustre, aero pbn.
2033 Feather, as 1155, in pbn.
2034-2035 Peacock feather, sgraf in: pbn, sb.
2036 Bud, in chin b with apri aero.
2037 Starburst, rbn & M&S o, apri aero.
2038-2039 Feather, sgraf in: pbn, sage.
2040 Feather, painted in sage.
2041 Peacock feather, sgraf in sage, pbn band.
2042 Patricia rose, with sage shaded band.
2043-2044 Aero in: sb, sb with pink line.
2045 Patricia rose, with sb aero.
2046 Aero in cela, lined with sage.
2047 Patricia rose, with cela aero.
2048 Aero in sage, with pbn line.
2049-2050 Bud, in: chin b, sage, aero pbn.
2051 Leaf, in pbn, aero pbn.
2052-2053 Bud, in: chg, pbn, aero in pbn.
2054-2055 Aero in: sage, pink.
2056 Band & cross, as 1452, chin b.
2057 Bands & spots.
2058 Aero in cela.
2059-2061 Patricia rose, aero inside in: pink, dark cela, reversed.
2062 Tree of life, sgraf in u-g band bn.
2063-2064 Patricia rose, b aero & line, reversed.
2065 Tree of life, sgraf in u-g old g & g, g tooth line.
2066 Chinese fern, sgraf in solid pink band.
2067 Starburst, in bn & g, solid old g band.
2068 Starburst, in bn & b, bk & pbn with wavy sgraf.
2069 Starburst, aero b sgraf, pbn in finish, as 2068.

1947
2070-2071 Scrolls, dashes & spots, in aero: pink, sage.
2072-2074 Bud & ring, sgraf in aero: sage, pink.
2075 Chinese fern, sgraf in u-g old g, leaves bn.
2076 Starburst, as 2069, aero pbn, b inside, 2076a no wavy band.
2077 Chinese feather, sgraf u-g in fern solid band, painted in bn.
2078 Tree of life, sgraf in pink u-g with bn leaves.
2079 Chinese feather & spots, in pbn.
2080 Bud & rings, sgraf in sb.
2081-2084 Leaf, sgraf & paint in: aero pink, sb, solid banded pink, sage.
2085-2089 Leaf, sgraf & paint in solid band of: bn, sb, sb with bk sgraf line, sage.
2090 Leaf & motif in bk, solid aero in old g.
2091 Tree of life, sgraf in solid b, u-g band, with bk.
2092 Leaf motif, sgraf in sb.
2093 Tree of life, sgraf in solid b, u-g band.
2094 Leaf motif, sgraf in pbn.
2095-2097 Leaf & spots as 2085, sgraf in: pbn, g, pink.
2098-2100 Swansea, litho bands in: sage, pink, chin b.
2101-2102 Tree of life, u-g in: g & bn, pink & g.
2103 Arab dhow boat motif, sgraf in solid b.
2104-2106 Arab dhow boat motif, in: pink with scroll border, old g with line, old g with scroll border.
2107 Aero sb with aero sage inside.
2108 Bud & rings, in mbn.
2109 Crescents, sgraf in aero chin b.
2110 Michaelmas, litho, fern border, aero g rim.
2111 Fern border, g rim, to match 2110.
2112 Michaelmas, aero pink, fern border.
2113 Fern border, to match 2112.
2114 Michaelmas, with sgraf ovals in g.
2115-2117 Not used.
2118-2121 Swansea, litho, aero in: cela, pink, apri, sb.
2122-2124 Dresden spray, aero in: sb, cela, pink.
2125 Not used.
2126-2127 Aero, as 2013, in: pink, jade.
2128 Not used.
1948
2130-2131 Patricia rose, sgraf in: jade, pink, fern.

2132-2133 Michaelmas, litho on edge, fern border.
2134-2135 Not used.
2136 Fern edge litho & sb.
2137-2138 Starburst, in aero: pbn, chin b.
2139 Tiger lily, with aero pomp.
2140 Winter leaf, hbn & bronze g, two leaves.
2141–2143 Feather & spots, as 1155, in: g, b, gy.
2144 Feather & spots, sgraf in aero chin b.
2145–2146 Swansea, graduated lines in: g, chin b.
2147-2148 Aero, as 2013, in: chin b, gy.
2149 Fern edge litho & rings with band of pink.
2150 Fern edge litho & rings with band of gy.
2151-2152 Bands (seconds) in: sage & pink, bn & pink.

1949
2153 Starburst, as 2137, in pink aero.
2154 Bud in sage, aero dark cela.
2155-2156 Aero, as 2013, in: lemon, chin b.
2157-2158 Feather, sgraf in aero: b, g.
2159 Patricia rose, band gy (US name 'Vogue Rose').
2160 Aero in g.
2161-2163 Starburst, b & pbn in aero: chin b, sage, sb.
2164 Fern border, aero in sb.
2165-2167 Starburst, sage & pink, aero in: sage, pink (spots bn), fern (spots pomp).
2168 Fern border with pink aero.
2169 Not used.
2170 Ladybird, sgraf in aero pomp.
2171 Ladybird, freehand, bk oval, pomp line.
2172 Fern in pomp, rings in bk.
2173 Clematis, with aero pomp.
2174 Ladybird, aero sb, painted in pomp.
2175 Scrolling with dashes & rings, sgraf in pomp.
2176-2179 Solid band in: chg, y, pomp, chin B&W.
2180 Tulip, in pomp.
2181 Pear, in pomp.
2182 Scrolling with dashes & rings, sgraf in fern.
2183 'Sabrina', freehand, 2-colour aero gy, pomp.
2184 'Sabrina', in aero gy, pomp.
2185 Aero, 2-colour, sb & pomp.
2186 Blue campanula, painted, aero gy.
2187 Canambola, aero in g, aero shaded edge & inside in pomp.
2188 English Summer, with fern border.
2189-2190 Solid bands in: gy, bronze g.
2191-2192 Long leaf, litho, bands in: sage & pink, gy & M&S o.
2193 Pink & gy leaf, with gy & sage bands.
2194 Pink & gy leaf, with sage & pink bands.

1950
2195-2198 Aero, 2-colour: gy & sbn, gy & y, gy & fern.
2199 Starburst, simple star, sgraf in aero sb, scallop border.
2200 Starburst, simple star, sgraf in aero b, scallop border.
2201 Fern border, gy aero.
2202 Starburst, aero chin b, pbn spots.
2203 Leaf, painted on 2-colour aero.
2204 Leaf, assorted aero g, gy, b.
2205 Printemps border, in b, Swansea litho centres.
2206 Starburst, simple star, sgraf in aero pbn.
2207 Oak leaf, chin b u-g, old g banding.
2208 Tulip, in bn & pink on u-g, old g banding.
2209 Oak leaf & sgraf, in u-g fern banding.
*2210 White dahlia (shaggy) in u-g fern, pink centre.
2211 Pear in pomp cups etc., aero y.
2212 Tulip in pomp cups etc., aero y.
2213 Pear in pomp cups etc., aero g.
2214 Tulip in pomp cups etc., aero g.
2215 Pear in pomp cups etc., aero chin b.
2216 Tulip in pomp cups etc., aero chin b.
2217 Leaf, paint & sgraf on u-g fern.
2218-2219 Ladybird, as 2170, but in: chin b, g.
2220-2221 Starburst, aero in: pink & scallop, sb & scallop.
2222 Oak leaf, in bk on u-g g.
2223-2225 Sea anemone, with: bn litho border, g shaded, pink shaded, on Kestrel.
2226 Calligraphic, in u-g g & old g, on hors d'oeuvres.
2227 Banded.
2228–2230 Banded & dontilled edge, as 2176, in: sky b, y g, sage.
2231 Wiped out waterlily, in old g.
2232 Ladybird, sgraf.
2233-2234 Star litho in b with: pomp band inside, chin b inside.
2235 Wiped out waterlily, in g band.
2236 Tree of life, aero in fern band.
2237 Aero, 2-colour, in sb & fern.
2238 Oak leaf, in u-g bk & old g, wavy border in b.
2239 Vegetable & fish subjects, u-g, on hors d'oeuvres.
2240 Leaves & flowers, u-g, in gs.
2241 Bud, stem sgraf on aero pomp, bk painted bud.
2242 Stylized leaf & microscope motifs, sgraf in g.
2243 Stylized fern, u-g in gs.
2244 Stylized fern, sgraf, as above.
2245 Stylized leaf, painted old g & g.
2246 Leaves, 4 sgraf leaves on cela.
2247 Leaf, sgraf on cela.
2248 Stylized fern, sgraf on old g.

1951
2249-2252 Scallop border, in fern & old g, with hand- painted: peach centre, apple centre, pear tree, fern leaf with b pods.
2253-2256 Scallop border, in bk, pink & old g, with hand-painted: fig centre, seaweed centre, centre in g & pink with bk dontils, centre in old g, fern, pink, y, g & bk.
2257 Leaf painted g & bn, on aero cela.
2258 Four leaves painted in bk, on aero g.
2259 Leaf freehand painted in bn, on aero cela.
2260-2264 Banded in: b, g, y, gyb, gy.
2265 Leaf painted in g & bn, on aero g.
2266-2268 Fern border, bands in: g, sb, mbn.
2269 Dahlia (shaggy), as 2210, in u-g bn.
2270 Wreath border, litho (Thos Hulmes).
2271 Tree of life, in u-g band of old g.
2272 Wiped out waterlily, in banded bn.
2273 Patricia rose, bn tooth litho border, on Kestrel.
2274 Banding, in pomp.
2275 Swansea litho, with b border.
2276 Bk leaf spray, scallop border.
2277 Pink & gy leaf litho, gy & M&S o bands.
2278 Azalea, two narrow bands in g.
2279 Azalea, one narrow band in g.

8 May 1952
2280-2281 Banding, u-g in: fern, old g.
2282-2283 Gardenia, bands in: wide sage, narrow sage.
2284 Magnolia, gy band.
2285 Clematis, sage band.
2286 Wreath border, two sage bands.
2287 Long leaf litho, two bands pink.
2288 Pink & gy leaf litho, two bands ag & gy.
2289 Blue star litho, colour edge in pomp.
2290 Bracken, leaf border in old g & g.
2291 Magnolia, with magnolia leaf border.
2292 Everlasting Life, border in bn & g.
2293-2294 Blue orchid, litho.

27 August 1953
2295 Azalea, wide bronze g band.
2296 Magnolia, wide gy band.
2297 Clematis, russet g band.
2298 Gardenia.
2299 Azalea.
2300 Clematis.

22 May 1954
2301 Beechwood.
2302 Gy leaf, pink & g narrow band.
2303 Clematis, wide sage band.

15 October 1955
2304 Wreath border.
2305 Richmond rose (made in England only).
2306-2309 Lines in: g, b, mbn, sage.

9 March 1956
2310 Blue orchid.
2311 Highland grass, u-g painted in bn & g. 16.06.56.
2312-2315 Crayon banding u-g in: fern with g crayon, bk with bk crayon, fern with bn crayon, g with b crayon. 02.07.56.
2316 As 1521, hbn & fern with sgraf.
2317 Blue fern, u-g painted in bn & b.

1957
2318 Sienna pastel in bn & bk litho.
2319 Olive pastel, u-g, litho.
2320 Blue pastel.
2321 Feather, in bk, litho.
2322 Stylized foliage.
2323-2328 Bk spot, rubber stamps & sgraf with band in: pbn, sev, pink, g, bk, chamise, on Kestrel.
2329-2334 Banded, in: pbn, b, pink, g, bk & chamise.
2335-2340 Star, rubber stamp, colours as above.
2341 Gardenia, sage shaded band.
2342 Azalea, bronze g shaded band.
2343 Clematis, bn shaded band.
2344 Magnolia, ag shaded band.
2345 Leaf centre.
2346 Petronella, litho.
2347 Brown peacock feather, litho.
2348 Peacock feather, litho.
2349-2350 Feather, u-g.
2351-2352 Bird, litho.
2353-2355 Leaf motif, in: bn, fern, charcoal bands.
2356-2361 Spirals, u-g banding in: charcoal, fern, bn, b, old g, fern.

August 1958
2362-2363 Crescents, sgraf in: sky b, sev.
2364 Sea anemone, bronze g band.
2365 Blue orchid, canton b band.
2366-2367 Not used.
2368-2369 Crescents, sgraf in: maize, cant.
2370 Meadowsweet.
2371 Carefree.
2372 Stylized leaf, freehand, u-g fern & maroon.
2373 Basque r, band in r, freehand leaf border in g.

January 1959
2374 Ferndown, freehand u-g.
2375 Hazelwood, u-g litho. 24.03.59.

2376 Feather, in g, u-g litho. 07.04 59.
2377 Marigold, freehand u-g. 21.04.59.
2378 Blue dahlia, freehand u-g.
2379 Acanthus, freehand u-g border.
2380 Simplicity.
2381 Hazelwood, u-g in bn (cc).
2382 Windfall, u-g freehand leaves. June 1959.
2383 Pink campion, u-g freehand.
2384 Blue orchid.
2385 Pink campion sidespray, u-g freehand. September 1959.
2386 Marigold, hand-painted u-g.
2387 Comfrey.
2388-2389 Camellia, finish in: elephant gy, moonstone gy.
2390 Candy stripes. December 1959.
2391 Gooseberry.
2392 New hat.
2393 Elderberry, freehand u-g pink & g, bands on edge.
2394 Pink campion centre spray.

January 1960
2395 Brushed-out border.
2396 Parrot tulips, litho tulips in pink, p, g.
2397 Grey leaf, Hyde Park bn band.
2398 Blue gentian.
2399 Acorn, ag band.
2400 Wavy litho border, in bn.
2401 Blue orchid.
2402 Patricia rose, russet band.
2403 Gooseberry, freehand centre.
2404 Meadowsweet.
2405 Gardenia.
2406 Tiger lily.

January 1961
2407 Beechwood, litho border.
2408 Banded u-g mushroom gy b.
2409 Gooseberry.
2410 Daffodil, u-g freehand. August 1961.
2411 Lily, u-g freehand painted.
2412 Swansea, litho.
2413 Blue dahlia.

April 1964
2414a-f Banding in: b, g, y, b dahlia, ferndown g, hazelwood bn.
2415-2416 Swansea centre, parrot tulip border.
2417 Floriana, u-g freehand, moonstone gy band.
2418 Fruit centre, coupe shape.
2419 Rhythm, freehand u-g.
2420 Diablo, cc.
2421 Square, in g & bn rubber stamp. March 1964.
2422 Ovals rubber stamp.
2423 Grecian (Lady Barbara), cc. June 1964.
2424 Penelope, cc.
2425-2428 Banding with dashes.
2429 Rubber stamp motif, cant & fern. 30.7.64.

CHINA

1951
1-6 Regency stripe, print & enamel, stripes with zig- zags, in r, g, old g & pomp, old g & g.
7-11 Sea anemone, aero & sgraf, crimson, jade, mbn, g.
11 Astral, aero, print & sgraf, lav.
12 Astral, s pink.
13-14 Not used.
15 Frond, on fern.
16 Leaves, aero pink & sgraf.
17 Panels, mbn aero, stars & wavy border sgraf.
18 Panels, aero in sang du boeuf (r).
19-21 Panels, bk wavy line sgraf cross-hatch, aero in: 19 sev, 20 mbn, 21 jade.
22 Not used.
23 Dahlia, shaggy motif, sgraf in u-g, old g band.
24 Wiped out waterlily, in u-g old g band, gilt.
25-30 Australian wild flower series: 25 Kangaroo paw, 26 Wanatah, 27 Hibiscus, 28 Bottle brush, 29 Spiderflower, 30 Passion flower, on champagne background.
31-36 As 25-30, on pink background.
37-42 As 25-30, on mixed g background.
43-48 As 25-30, on lav background.
49-54 As 25-30, on gyb background.
55-60 Not used.
61-66 English wild flower series: 61 Bindweed, 62 Speedwell, 63 Solomon's seal, 64 Thistle, 65 Dandelion, 66 Coltsfoot, on champagne background.
67-72 As 61-66, on s pink background.
73-78 As 61-66, on mixed g background.
79-84 As 61-66, on lav background.
85-90 As 61-66, on gyb background.
91-96 As 61-66, on sb background.
97-101 Swansea Printemps, litho sprays alternate panels in: 97 sev, 98 mbn, 99 lav, 100 gyb, 101 fern.
102 Not used.
103-105 Sea anemone, aero & sgraf, sev, fern, gb.
106 Not used.
107-113 Nutmeg tree, aero & sgraf, in crimson, jade, mbn, g, sev, fern, gyb.

114 Not used.
115-121 Persian rose, aero, sgraf & painted, crimson, jade, mbn, g, sev, fern, gyb.
122 Not used.
123-125 Wreath litho, aero in: 124 pink, 125 apri.
126 Not used.
127 Litho spray border.
128-132 Not used.
133 Star litho, in sb, on Countess shape.
134 Star litho, gold spots between, on Quail.
135-142 Not used.
143 Floral litho, lav with sgraf.
144-148 Not used.
149-154 Sgraf motif, aero in: lav, gb, pink, sev, mbn, fern.
155-156 Astral, as C11, in: gyb, sev.
157-159 Not used.
160-164 Gold motifs, with scallop border, in: mbn, sev, gyb, fern, jade.
165-166 Not used.
167 Tulip, freehand, bn print u-g etched.
168 Wreath border, sage lines.
169 Blue star litho, chin b band & gold.
170-172 Daisy centre, Princess shape, alternate panels u-g, aero in: mbn, gyb, gold.
173-175 Not used.
176 Orchid, in-g print & freehand finish gold.
177 Tiger lily, in-g print, in: g, y, pink, bns.
178 Regency stripe, bk wavy line, sgraf swirls.
179-182 Orchid print, in-g aero in: pink, fern, mix g, 182a chart.
183-186 Tulip, in-g print in: pink, gyb, fern & mauve.
187-190 Tiger lily, in-g print, aero in: fern, pink, gyb & g.
191-194 Orchid, in-g print in y with aero in: fern, gyb, lav, chart.
195-198 Tulip, in-g print in old g, aero in: fern, gyb, pink, chart.
199-202 Tiger lily, in-g print in bn, aero in: fern, gyb, pink, chart.
203 Tulip, in-g print in old g.
204 Orchid, in-g print in old g.
205 Tiger lily, in-g print in old g.
206 Floral, in u-g pink & mbn with sgraf.
207 Floral, in gyb.
208-209 Tulip, in-g print, aero in: lav, g.
210 English wildflower second series, u-g print in old g & freehand painted peasblossom, cornflower, buttercup, marigold.
211 English wildflower series, as 210, bn print.
212-213 Sunflower, print & paint in y & bn, print in: old g, bn u-g.
214 Gardenia, print with sage aero & gold.
215 Magnolia, print, gy band & gold.
216 Azalea, print, bronze g band & gold.
217 Clematis, print, sage band & gold.
218 Wreath border, on Princess, gold line.
219-224 Thrush, old g bird, print, wavy border & gold, aero in: sev, fern & chart, mbn & g, fern & chart, mbn, sev.
225 Cockerel, old g print & paint, aero mbn.
226-228 Pheasant, print in old g & paint, aero in: jade, fern, sev.
229-230 Peacock, print in old g, aero in: mbn, s pink.
231-236 Regency stripe, print old g, aero in: s pink no gold, g, gyb, lav, gy, apri.
237-242 Regency stripe, old g coloured handles pink, mix g, sb, lav, gy, apri.
243 Tiger lily, old g print, fern paint.
244 Tiger lily, fern bn print, old g paint.
245-248 Aero, in: pink, gyb, mix g, jade with gold edges.
249-251 Orchid, as 191, aero in: pink, mix g, sage.
252 Tulip, as 183, aero mix g.
253 Orchid, as 179, aero lav.
254 Tiger lily, as 187, aero chart.
255 Tulip, as 183, aero chart.
255a Orchid, as 191, aero mix g.
256-258 Regency feather, in: avocado & myrtle g.
259 Pink Pride, litho bud motifs avocado.
260 Spring Pride, litho with avocado.
261 Autumn Pride, litho with myrtle g.
262-264 Spiral fern, litho with: crimson, avocado, myrtle g. 'Ivory size wash on china creates matching background with earthenware' (sic).

1952
265 Blue star, gold finish, as C169.
266 Wreath border, as C123, sage band.
267 Gardenia, as C214, sage & gold band.
268 Magnolia, as C215, gy & gold band.
269 Azalea, as C216, bronze g & gold line.
271 Pink Pride, as C259, pink aero inside.
272 Sping Pride, as C260, fern.
273 Autumn Pride, as C261, sb.
274 Gardenia, mbn band, bronze g band.
275 Magnolia, size washed bodies, bn band.
276 Azalea, mbn band.
277 Clematis, russet g band.
278 Gardenia, sage band.
279 Magnolia, fern band.
280 Azalea, size wash but for coffee/tea pots.
281 Clematis, ag band.
282-287 Sunflower, u-g print & freehand, aero in: mbn, jade, sage, sb, sev, gyb. Gold line.
288 Not used.
289 Sunflower, u-g print & freehand, aero chart.

290 Not used.
291 Magnolia.
293 Azalea, bronze g finish.
294 Clematis, ag finish.
295-304 Gardenia, with aero colour wiped from litho, aero in: mbn, chart, sage, sb, pink, gyb, fern, pastel g, lav, jade.
305 Blue star, litho, band chin b. C/E265 (sic).
306-312 Sunflower, in bn u-g with aero in: mbn, jade, sage, sb, sev, gyb, chart.
313 Not used.
314-323 Magnolia, with aero colour wiped away from litho, aero in colours as 306-312.
324-333 Azalea, with aero colour wiped away from litho, aero in colours as 306-312.
334-343 Clematis, with aero colour wiped away from litho, aero in colours as 306-312.
344-353 Gardenia, with gold & dark band of colour, aero colour wiped away from litho, aero in: mbn, sage, ag, bronze g, gy, pink, fern, russet, b.
354-361 Magnolia, with gold & band, aero colour wiped away from litho, aero in: mbn, sage, ag, bronze g, gy, pink, fern, russet g.
362-363 Not used.
364-372 Azalea, with gold & band, aero colour wiped away from litho, aero in colours as 344-352.
373 Not used.
374-381 Clematis, with gold & band, aero colour wiped from litho, aero in colours as 344-352.
382-383 Not used.
384-385 Blue star, litho, mbn band, no band.
386-387 Chrysanthemum, old g finish, aero in: jade, gyb.
388 Chrysanthemum, bn print, aero sb.
389 Not used.
390 Blue star, litho, band mbn.
391 Pink Pride, solid pink inside.
392 Not used.
393-399 Orchid, u-g print with aero colour wiped away from litho, aero in: mbn, jade, chart, sage, sev, gyb, sb.
400-406 Orchid, old g print with aero colour wiped away from litho, aero in colours as 393-399.
407-413a Tiger lily, bn print with aero colour wiped away from litho, aero in: mbn, jade, chart, sage, sev, gyb, sb, pastel g.
414-420a Tiger lily, old g print with aero colour wiped away from litho, aero in: mbn, jade, chart, sage, sev, gyb, sb, fern.
421-427 Tulip, bn u-g print with aero colour wiped away from litho, aero in colours as 400-406.
428-434 Tulip, old g u-g print with aero colour wiped away from litho, aero in colours as 421-427.

1953
435 Gardenia, as C214 without gold.
436 Magnolia, as C215 without gold.
437 Azalea, as C216 without gold.
438 Clematis, as C217 without gold.
439 Not used.
440 Rose & leaves.
441-446 Aero with stippled gold edge (clearance lines) in: fern, sev, mbn, jade, gyb, pink.
447 Roosters, print bk, paint y, scarlet, bn, gy.
448-451 Roosters, as 447, band all over wiped away from litho in: fern, sage, chart, mbn.
452 Cockerel, print in bk, colour as 447.
453-456 Cockerel, as 452, band all over wiped from litho in: fern, sage, chart, mbn.
457-460 Pink Pride, band in: mbn, fern, ag, sage.
461 Green star, print, band in russet & gold.
462-463 Blue star, band in: pink, ag.
464 Gold star, stamped in gold, b band.
465-469 Gold star, aero in: mbn, jade, chart, fern, gyb.
470 Gardenia, without gold.
471 Magnolia, without gold.
472 Azalea, without gold.
473 Clematis, without gold.
474 Wreath border, sky b bands.
475 Regency feather, avocado finish.
476-477 Not used.
478-483 Magnolia, wide band & narrow band in: gy & g, sage & hbn, mbn & hbn, pink & gy, hbn & bronze g, russet & hbn.
484 Wreath border, sky b band.
485 Fragrance, floral litho.
486 Wild strawberry, litho border.
487 Floris, floral litho & border.
488 Pink Pride, with jade band.
489-496 Gardenia, Magnolia, Azalea, Clematis, Gardenia, Magnolia, Azalea, Clematis, no gold finish.
497 Blue orchid litho, wide hbn band.
498-499 Blue orchid, bands in: b & hbn, gyb & hbn.
500 Wreath border, without gilt decoration.
501 Raised spot, aero in pink & painted.
502-505 Not used.
506 Raised spot, in cela.
507 Green star, banded in pink.
508 Not used.
509 Green star, fern edge line.
510-511 Not used.

512-513 Raised spot in: lemon, glad g.
514-519 Not used.
520-527 Leaves border litho with aero in: pink, chart, jade, gyb, sage, cela, lemon, glad g.

1954
528-534 Swirl, raised enamel tailed spot in: s pink, chart, jade, gyb, cela, lemon, glad g.
535 Star litho, as C134 without spots.
536-541 Gardenia, no gold finish, with aero colour wiped from litho, aero in: chart, sage, pink, gyb, fern, chin b.
542-547 Magnolia, with aero colour wiped away from litho, aero in: chart, sage, pink, gyb, fern, chin b.
548-553 Azalea, with aero colour wiped away from litho, aero in: chart, sage, pink, gyb, fern, chin b.
554-559 Clematis, with aero colour wiped away from litho, aero in: chart, sage, pink, gyb, fern, chin b.
560 Star in b, banded in old g.
561-566 Raised spot and band: gy spot & mix gy band, glad g spot & band, scarlet spot & sb band, fern spot & band, dark b spot & mixed gy band, mbn spot & band.
567 Rings & spots, raised, in slate gy.
568 Not used.
569-571 Rings & spots: scarlet aero with sb band, spruce g aero with bronze g band, lg aero with fern band.
572 Not used.
573-574 Swirl in: pink, scarlet with sb band.
575-576 Not used.
577-578 Swirl in: fern, gy.
579-584 Raised spot, as 501, aero in: sev, mbn, jade, chart, fern, gyb.
585-590 Swirl, sgraf, aero in colours as 579-584.
591-596 Gold Pride, stamp in gold, colours as above.
597-598 Raised spot, in: gyb, jade.

1955
599 Pink Pride, litho all over.
600 Pink Pride, with narrow mbn band.
601-605 Aero, 2-colour, in: sev & mbn, gy & fern, fern & mbn, gyb & navy b, sage & mbn.
606 Gold star.
607 Gold Pride, aero s pink.
608-611 Whispering grass litho in: fern, gyb, sev, mbn.
612-615 One o'clocks litho in: fern, gyb, sev, mbn.
616-619 Magnolia litho, aero background in: tan, gyb, cela, glad g.
620 Not used.
621-622 Parrot tulip litho, 622 litho with sage litho border.
623-631 Aero with dontil edge, substandard ware, aero in: pink, jade, gyb, cela, lemon, glad g, sev, mbn, fern.
632-637 Green star litho, aero in: scarlet, bk, mbn, chart, fern, gyb.
638-643 Pink Pride, with band in: pink, ag, sage, fern, old g, gyb.
644-647 Parrot tulip, with shaded border in: bronze g, sage, gyb, pink.
648-651 Not used.
652-658 Scroll sgraf in: sev, mbn, jade, bk, fern, gyb, pink.
659-664 Two lines & circles, sgraf in aero: pink, gyb, sev, lemon, mbn, bk.
665-671 Not used.
672-673 Green star with areo in: pink, glad g.
674 Blue gentian & litho border.
675 Blue orchid.
676-677 Raised spot in: lemon, s pink.
678 Swirl, aero navy b & raised swirl.
679-689 Ring & dot, sgraf with hbn band, aero in: pink with bk band, gyb, sev, chart, mbn, bk, lav, cant, forest g, fern, jade.
690 Not used.
691-701 Bud, sgraf in aero: pink, gyb, sev, chart, mbn, bk, lav, cant, forest g, fern, jade.
702 Not used.

1956
703 Swirl, sgraf in aero blueberry.
704-715 Rings, sgraf, aero in: s pink, gyb, sev, chart, mbn, bk, lav, cant, forest g, fern, jade, charcoal.
716-727 Vertical line with dashes, sgraf, aero in colours as 704-715.
728-739 Scallop, sgraf, aero in colours as 704-715.
740-745 Shaggy motif, sgraf in aero: gyb, mbn, fern, charcoal, chart, sev.
746-751 Astral, with small sgraf rings, aero in: gyb, fern, sev, charcoal, tan, terracotta.
752-757 Stylized tulip, sgraf in aero: gyb, bk, chart, s pink, fern, mbn.
758-763 Fern, sgraf, aero in colours as 752-757.
764-769 Leaf, sgraf, aero in colours as 753-757.
770-773 Scroll, as 652 aero in: chart, lav, cant, forest g.
774 Not used.
775-778 Serpentine line (wavy line), sgraf in aero: tan, gyb, fern, mbn.
779-782 Serpentine line & fern leaf, sgraf in aero: tan, gyb, fern, mbn.
783-786 Serpentine lines with hatched centres, sgraf in aero: tan, gyb, fern, mbn.
787-790 Serpentine lines with spot & crescent centres, sgraf in aero: tan, gyb, fern, mbn.
791-794 Sgraf in serpentine moulding
799-802 Bud & spot, sgraf in aero, serpentine moulding.
803 Lines & circles, sgraf.
804 Leaf border litho.
805 Charcoal feather litho.

1957
806-811 Corinthian, sgraf in broad band & gold.

812-813 Not used.
814 Romanesque, sgraf border in cbn with gold line.
815 Romanesque, sgraf border in bk with gold line.
816-817 Not used.
818 Shaggy motif, sgraf in jade aero.
819 Sheraton, sgraf border in mbn with gold line.
820 Palladian, sgraf border in fern band with gold line.
821-822 Spiral fern, as 262, in: resida g.
823 Not used.
824 Pomme d'or, gold apple painted, later cc.
825-828 Painted feather, aero & painted in: b, gyb with sgraf.
829a-i Square in bk, with 4 sgraf lines finished with gold rings, aero in: s pink, jade, mbn, fern, bk, gyb, sev, chart, forest g, cant.
830 Not used.
831a-i Aero, colours as 829a-i, on Fluted.
832a-i Aero, colours as 829a-i, on low Fluted.
833a-i Aero, colours as 829a-i, on Fluted.
834a-i Aero & gold line with raised spot, colours as 829a-i.
835a-i Aero & gold stamp, colours as 829a-i.
836 Gold star with gold edge, on Fluted.
837 Gold stamp, on Fluted.
838 Spiral, fern litho in b.
839 Swirl, sgraf in aero pink.
840-845 Confetti, aero, sgraf squares, stamped rings.
846 Gold star, as 464, aero inside in mbn.
847-852 Green star, banded, no gold.
853 Relief polka dots, pink freehand spots.
854-858 Relief polka dots, freehand spots.
859-864 Shaded border & raised spot, harlequin-style open stock.
865-868 Parrot tulip, shaded band & gold line.
869-870 Wavy vertical bands, as 775.
871 Not used.
872-873 Teazle, printed, with old g banding.
874-877 Aero, on Fluted.
878 Raised spot in gy.
879-884 Green star, as 484, various banded colours.
885-890 Aero with gold line finish.
891 Parrot tulip & litho border.
892 Floris with gilt border.
893-898 Black fruit, printed, subjects: pear, grape, strawberry, apple, peach, cherry.

October 1958
899 Susie Cooper's Black & Whites, cc bk fruit subjects with bk banding, on saucers.
900 Springtime, printed wreath border.
901 Virginia, printed floris border.
902-907 Shaded bands & raised spots, various colours, sold as harlequin sets.
908 Blue ivy, cc in b with gold line.
909-911 Romance, cc pink floral spray, shaded band.
912 Hyde Park, cc leaves in bns with gold line.
913 Sepia rose, cc bn floral aero & gold line.
914-917 Magnolia, aero & gold line.
918-919 Springtime, floral wreath border band & gold.
920-921 Patricia rose, cc floral banded.
922 Relief border motif in terracotta, gold, on Fluted.
923 Simple bud motif on border, relief deco.
924 Bud motif, simple dashes & spot in relief.
925 Two dashes & spot motif in relief.
926 Gold & gy band, with white relief spot on gold.
927 Gold & g band, relief white spots on verge.
928-929 Marguerite, cc floral in b & bn band in g & gold.
930-935 Gold star, various colour finish.
936-941 Aero, on Fluted.
942-943 Gold line, on Fluted.
944 Not used.
945-950 Simplicity, freehand floral motif with sgraf.
951 Gold line decoration, on Fluted.
952-953 Sepia rose, cc with aero in sandalwood.
954 Gold line decoration, on Fluted.
955-958 Simplicity, freehand floral motif with sgraf.
959 Raised spot with bk aero.
960-961 Gold line decoration, on Fluted.
962-964 Parrot tulip, small shaded band & gold line.
965 Magnolia, large spray with aero.
966 Blue orchid, large spray with aero.
967 Sepia rose, large spray with aero.,
968 Clematis, aero in g.
969 Gardenia, large spray, aero in b.
970 Parrot tulip, aero in g, band in pink.
971 Sepia rose motif in cup, with banding.
972 Blue orchid motif in cup, with banding in b, as 345.
973 Banded in b.
974 Accolade litho, border best gold.
975 Crack willow, cc wheat & leaves with gold line.
976 White bryony, cc border motifs with silver line.
977 Candide, cc floral in bn.
978 Sweet chestnut, cc floral centre spray.

November 1959
979-980 White jasmine, floral spray & banding.
981 Day lily, floral spray in bn, band in g, gold line.
982 Grey leaves, band in bn with gold line.
983 Lady smock, floral spray in g, o, y, banded finish & gold.

984 Heliobore (sic), floral print in peach, gold line.
985 Cornflower, side spray print in y, bn, pink, g.
986 Blush rose, floral print in b, gy, band in g.
987 Wild rose, floral print, band in g.
988 Sepia rose, blueberry aero, gold line.
989 Accolade, sgraf border, aero in g.
990 (Vista) Classic Vista architectural print in tan & various colours.
991 Margaret rose, cc floral in b & pink, gold line.
991a Margaret rose, cc, on different shape (sic).
992-997 Simple flower motif, paint & sgraf on aero.
998-1003 Grapevine motif, sgraf on aero.
1004-1005 Accolade, as C989, sgraf, aero in: terracotta, sev.
1006 Elderberry, border print.
1007 Blue vine, cc border silver line.
1008 Azalea, low new shape.
1009 Clematis.
1010 Assyrian motif, cc in fawn & gy.

April 1960
1011 Blue forget-me-not, printed floral.
1012 Speedwell, floral centre print with gold line.
1013 Margaret rose, floral with no finish.
1014 Jasmine spray, with b aero.
1015-1016 Wild rose, floral print with aero.
1017 Christmas rose, with border in pink.
1018 Cornflower, with border in pink.
1019-1022 Star in g & bands.
1023 Flower motif, as 992, g aero.
1024 Clematis, band in pink & gold.
1025 Azalea, band in pink & gold.
1026 Blue orchid, band in b.
1027 Gardenia.
1028 Wild rose.
1029-1030 Magnolia.
1031 Gy leaves, with band & gold line.
1032 Christmas rose, with pink shaded band.
1033 Lady smock, shaded band in g.
1034 Golden rose, cc with band & gold line.
1035 Glen mist, cc floral in b & gy with b band.
1036-1039 Gold leaf, stamped with aero & gold line.
1040-1045 Gold star, with aero & gold line.
1046 Golden thistle, cc gold motifs & aero.
1047 Gold garland, cc gold motifs.
1048 Circles, sim. to Astral, aero in bn.
1049-1050 Gold & bk scroll, cc border.
1051 Blue vine, border only.
1052 Blue ivy, no finish, on Fluted.
1053 Christmas rose.
1054 Universal fruit, cc aero in 6 colours.
1055 Constable Scenes & London Cries, cc 6 colours.
1056 English country scenes & gems, cc 6 colours.
1057 Japanese & Clipper series, cc 6 colours.
1058 Gold & bk leaf, baroque leaf.
1059 Gold & bn leaf & flourish.
1060 Golden wheat.
1061 Not used.
1062-1063 Patricia rose, with banding.
1064-1065 Swansea spray, with banding.
1066 Floris, band in g & gold line.
1067 Wreath border, band in g.
1068 Romance, with b vine border.
1069-1070 Margaret rose, paint & sgraf.
1071-1076 Flower motif, as 992.
1077 Aero in pink.
1078 Not used.
1079 Fluted shape, with platinum edge.
1080 Floral prints, with size wash & gold line.
1081-1084 Floral prints, with aero & gold line.
1085 Gold bud, stamped motif with aero.
1086-1088 Floral, cc.

February 1961
1089 Traditional floral, cc, Hampton & Cambridge shapes.
1090-1091 Gold garland.
1092 Floral chintz sprig.
1093 Floral chintz spray panels.
1094 Framed, traditional floral, cc.
1095a-c Debonair spray, size wash various colours.
1096 Gold border, cc, on Fluted.
1097 Litho border sample.
1098-1099 Traditional sprays in aero panels.
1100-1107 Traditional floral lithos in sgraf panels.
1108 Gold border, scalloped.
1109 Romance shaded band & gold line, 5 variants.
1110 Traditional floral litho.
1111-1113 Gold panels, print & aero.
1114 Margaret rose, pink band & gold line.
1115-1117 Not used.
1118-1123 Blue star, banding in various colours.
1124 Golden wheat, cc, for Fondeville. 31.08.61.
1125 Turq & gold scroll, cc, for Fondeville.
1126 Gold thistle, cc, for Fondeville.
1127 Sepia rose.
1128 Eternal youth, floral, no gold line.
1129 White jasmine, shaded band in pink.

1130 Gy leaves, with y size wash.
1131 Lady-smock, gold line.
1132 Christmas rose, shaded band in pink.
1133 White jasmine, gold line.
1134 Gy leaves, gold line.
1135 Lady-smock, gold line.
1136 Christmas rose.

October 1961
1137 Rosemary, cc floral aero in b & gold line.
1138 Floral spray, cc scallop border, aero pink.
1139 Talisman, cc floral in g, pink, with banded finish.
1140-1141 Aero.
1142 Aero & floral spray inside.
1143 Musical instruments, cc motifs.
1144 Scallop edge, 4 designs with aero in 4 colours.
1145 Dianthus, floral with gy aero, on Can.
1146 Border in g & bn with gold line.
1147-1148 French edge & line in platinum.
1149 Vine leaf border.
1150 Dawn rose, cc floral & gold line, for South Africa.
1151 French edge line.
1152 Pink rose, cc aero in b.
1153 Blue rose, cc aero in b (1153-1159 Cx numbers perhaps for export).
1154 Marguerite, gold line.
1155 Sepia rose, aero & banding.
1156 Blue vine.
1157 Elderberry, gold line.
1158 Blue vine, colour variant.
1159 Elderberry, no gold line.
1160 Katina (Godilia), cc floral y, g, gy with band.
1161 Pomme d'or, with cant band.
1162 Platinum line.
1163 Blue peony, cc floral in b.
1164 Melody, cc musical instruments, a-e aero variants.
1165 Bridal bouquet, cc floral pink, b, gy, fern border.
1166 Regency stripe, cc panels with bands, on Fluted, 6 colours a-f, for Cassidy's, Canada.
1167 Margaret rose, gold line.
1168 Floral & aero in old g.
1169 Aero & sgraf. 1167-1169 for Cassidy's, Canada, on traditional Kent shape.
1170 Blue rose, Kent shape selection.
1171 Flower motif for Cassidy's, Canada.
1172 Floral centres in tea sets, parrot tulip, gardenia, sepia rose, clematis, magnolia, azalea, band & wipe from litho.
1173-1174 Regency stripe, without gold line.
1175-1176 Simplicity, freehand floral on aero.
1177 Form & colour, aero inside hollow ware, in plum.
1178 Cornflower, aero in bn & band b.
1179 Regency stripe, 6 colours.
1180 Margaret rose, platinum line, 5 piece setting.
1181 Bridal bouquet, platinum line, Quail & Rutland.
1182-1183 Arricula, cc floral, in: g & y.
1184 Accolade litho, border in platinum.
1185-1187 Aero, on Fluted, in: oak apple, mistletoe g, coffee bn.
1188-1193 Marguerite, aero inside in 6 colours.
1194-1199 Dahlia, cc floral, aero inside in 6 colours.
2000-2001 Indian fern, cc, 2000 with gold trim, 2001 without trim.
2002 Sunflower print, with aero & band.
2003 Golden glade, verge leaf border in gold, on Fluted.
2004 Silver oak leaf, printed band & aero.
2005 Lady Barbara, cc tulip border, g band & silver line.
2006 Penelope, cc stylized border, silver line.
2007 Penelope, without silver.
2008-2009 Not used.
2010 Christmas rose, y line at edge.
2011-2012 Floral, in bk & b cc, gold line.
2013 Bridal bouquet.
2014-2015 Flower motif, freehand & gold line.
2016 White wedding, cc centre spray in pink, gy, b.
2017 Mobiles.
2018 Apple Gay, cc border motifs in b, r, g.
2019 Persia, cc motifs in vertical panels, banded.
2020 Braemar, cc floral in b.
2021 Rothesay, cc floral band in gy.
2022 Banding, with gold line.
2023 Spiral fern, in avocado g.
2024-2025 Combined Braemar & Rothesay motifs.
2026 Black fruit, cc as 893, no finish.
2027-2028 Bridal bouquet, 2028 old g.
2029 Aero, 6 colours.
2030 Braemar.
2031 Grandeur, cc border in best gold & lime band.
2032 Abstract, clusters of blobs in bk & taupe.
2033 Black banding, with various colours aero.
2034 Broken stripes, scratched lines in 6 aero colours, as Harlequin set.
2035 Blue peony.
2036 Margaret rose, band in b.
2037 Vintage, cc floral dash handles.
2038 Nasturtium, cc floral in g, r, bn.
2039 Venetia, cc stylized leaf scrolls in old g, bn.
2040 Moselle, cc leaf border o, bn, g.

2041 Flower motif, no freehand.
2042 Engagement, platinum line to edge & verge.
2043 Mayfair, liquid gold line.
2044 Sepia rose.
2045 Romance, band in b.
2046 Gardenia.
2047 Blush rose, band in b.
2048 Chatsworth, cc border, g line at edge.
2049 Braemar.
2050 Rothesay, band in b.
2051 Teazle, band in maize.
2052 Marguerite, band in gy.
2053 Azalea, terracotta finish.
2054 Romance, aero in 6 colours.
2055 Reverie, cc floral b.
2056 Corinthian, cc stylized leaf motifs bn & bk.
2057 Pomegranate, cc stylized floral, bn aero.
2058 Ram, cc centre & border.
2059 Gy leaves, aero in y.
2060 Blush rose, aero & band in b.
2061 Lady smock, aero & band in g.
2062 Gy leaves, aero & band.
2063 Magnolia, litho & banded.
2064 Classic band, in old g with gy scrolling.
2065 Whispering grass, b, in hollow ware.
2066 One o'clocks, aero in b.
2067 Braemar, aero in bk.

December 1965
2068 Contrast, aero in bk matt.
2069 Contrast, aero in bk matt, sponged motifs.
2070 Garland, floral, sponged in bn & bk, aero in bn.
2071 Art Nouveau, cc floral in bn.
2072 Art Nouveau, cc floral in b.
2073 Autumn leaves & berry, cc motifs, old g line.
2074-2075 Floral in frame cc.
2076 Jason, with burnished gold, on Fluted.

January 1966
2077 Magnolia.
2078 Blue peony, band in gy.
2079 Cinderella, plain white, on Fluted.
2080-2081 Distinctive, motifs on edge in white.
2082 Clematis.
2083 Magnolia, band in g.
2084 Parrot tulip.
2085 Clematis, band in g.
2086 Blue gentian, band in gy.
2087 Iris, cc floral, band in g.
2088 Carnation, cc floral in b & band.
2089 Solera, cc floral, aero, band & gold line decoration.
2090 Bn rubber stamp motif with b spots.
2091 Spiral fern, in g.
2092 Bridal bouquet, with band.
2093 Pirouette, white spiral backstamp only.
2094 Forest, aero in matt g.
2095 Amber, aero in old g.

2096 Rosemary decoration, best gold lines.
2097 Pimento, aero in matt o.
2098 Rothesay, cc with aero.
2099 Braemar, aero & banded.
2100 Cornflower.
2101 Champagne.
2102 Pimpernel.
2103 Mariposa border, cc floral in y, bn, bk with gold.
2104 Mercury, cc motifs in vertical stripes in b.
2105 Neptune, cc motifs in vertical stripes in g.
2106 Andromeda, cc motifs in vertical stripes in r.
2107 Saturn, cc motifs in vertical stripes in bn.

January 1968
2108 Gold flower heads, band & aero.
2109 Aero, in old g band & best gold line.
2110-2113 Heraldry, cc in: bk, r, old g, g.
2114 Carnaby daisy, cc matt & gloss in various colours.
2115-2118 Harlequinade, cc overlapping blob shapes b, g, o, bk, y, pink.

May 1968
2119-2124 Chatsworth, cc various colours.
2125-2126 Chatsworth, with gold line.
2127-2128 Vintage, with gold line.
2129-2130 Autumn leaves, cc stylized & gold line.
2131-2134 Keystone, matt cc border in: bk, r, o gold, g.
2135-2138 Nebula, cc abstract swirl in gloss pimento on matt aero in: bk, pimento, forest g, amber.
2139-2140 Enchantment, cc floral, size wash & gold line.
2141-2146 Gay stripes, multi-coloured banding.
2147 Dumbbells, cc motifs old g & r.
2148 Mulberry, with aero.
2149 Kingfisher, with aero.
2150 Diablo, cc double teardrop motifs old g & bk.
2151 Pennant, cc E shapes in gloss b on various matt aero colours.
2152-2153 Day lily, cc with banding.
2154-2155 Wild rose, cc with banding.
2156-2157 Blush rose, cc with banding.
2158 Classic, with old g.
2159 Athena, in g.
2160 Hyde Park, with banding.
2161-2162 Romance, with banding.

October 1969
2163 Illusion, band in platinum.
2164 Reflection, band in platinum.
2165 Colosseum, cc matt bk border, gold line & aero.
2166 Florida, cc two flowers in turq & beige.
2167 Pinnochio.
2168 Satellite, as 2163 in gold.
2169 Saturn, as 2164 in gold.
2170 Vintage, with banded decoration.

January 1971 onwards (entries undated)
2171 Autumn leaves, cc with banding.
2172 Cressida, chevron border.
2173 Sparta, chevron stylized leaf border in bk.
2174 Columbine, wavy lines border in g, r, bn.

2175 Blue gentian, with banding.
2176 Cornpoppy, print in r, bn, bk.
2177-2182 Camellia, floral motifs.
2183 Aero decoration.
2184 Charisma, bands in silver & bk.
2185 Indian summer, banded in r & bk.
2186 Everglade, banded in g & o.
2187-2188 Lucerne, banded b & bk.
2189 Aero, various colours for Harlequin set.
2190 Tiger lily.
2191 Black-eyed Susan, cc floral in o & b.
2192 Band of o border.
2193 Prelude, bands of bn & matt bk.
2194 Banded in g & bk.
2195-2196 Banding.
2197 Blue anemone, cc floral p, pink & bk.
2198-2203 Exotic wild flowers used for World Wildlife Fund designs.
2204 Colosseum, with badge motif.
2205 Persia, with badge motif.
2206 Ashmun, cc stylized ancient Egyptian subjects, in b & bn (Thebes variation in bns & rs).
2207 Chou Dynasty, stylized creatures, cc in b & bn.
2208 Floral bouquet, litho of g, y, o, flowers with background in printed silver lustre (limited edition of 500 for silver wedding anniversary of Queen Elizabeth & Prince Philip).
2209 Floral bouquet, litho of g, y, o, flowers with background in printed silver lustre (limited edition of 500 for the silver jubilee of Queen Elizabeth).

April 1977
2210 English wild flower series, cc.

1979
2211 Birds of the world, cc birds such as American redstart, b throat redstart, g goldfinch etc.
2212 Iris, cc in b.
2213-2214 Floral, cc with silver lustre.
2215 Not used.
2216 Honey rose.
2217 Fritillary Blue.
2218 Tobacco Brown.
2219 Cocoa Brown.

Adams Patterns
Two designs produced between 1967-1969 for Adams: Greensleeves & Blue Mantle.
1982
Meadowlands for Boots.
1983
Blue Daisy, printed flower motifs in diaper.
Daisy pink, version of above for the French market.
Stardust, star motifs.
April.
Inspiration, for Tesco (known as Arrowheads until production).
Blue Polka Dot, despatched August 1983 for Tiffany's, New York.
Blue Haze, 1984, banded in b & bn.
Florida, 1985, cc floral in pink, bk, g, r, p, bn.

Susie Cooper used hundreds of different shapes in her career. In the early days of her business, wares from several potteries were used, making identification extremely complex. For instance, shapes decorated during her period with Wood's included ashtrays, vinegar bottles, chamber pots, tiny butter pats and at least twelve different forms of lamp stand. The shapes listed below are the principal ones used in her own production, listed in order of appearance.

Kestrel

The 'Kestrel' shape for many epitomizes the design of Susie Cooper; this is perhaps unsurprising given that it was used for nearly thirty years. Coffee and tea pots were exhibited for the first time at the British Industries Fair in 1932, with the full range being introduced gradually over the next few years. The 'Kestrel' cover dish appeared in 1933, and was patented in that year because of its great success. It appears that Susie refined the 'Kestrel' tea and coffee pot shapes, since some early examples have a more pronounced domed cover. A tea cup with the distinctive 'Kestrel' shape, flared rim and downward sloping handle was produced in small quantities c. 1932–1933. It was prone to thermal shock during firing and therefore suffered high losses. Instead of tampering with the design, Susie ceased production and used the standard Wood's shape called 'Regina' to complement her 'Kestrel' pots. Wood's own patterns were also applied to Susie Cooper shapes such as 'Kestrel'.

Curlew

The 'Curlew' shape, exhibited for the first time in February 1933, was probably designed late in 1932. The radically streamlined body of the 'Curlew' tea pot, like that of the 'Kestrel' shape, is reminiscent of the avant-garde sculpture of the late nineteen-twenties. 'Curlew' tureens have a particularly dramatic and stylized organic profile, even without the dual-purpose lid.

Wren

The 'Wren' shape was probably designed by Susie Cooper late in 1934; it was shown for the first time at the Royal Academy exhibition of February 1935 to great acclaim. Susie had been commissioned by Wood & Sons to produce a shape specially for the company. The result was a combination of organic lines and streamlined flourishes. The light incisions into the surface of the pots were of particular interest to the press at the time; a review in *The Pottery and Glass Record* explained, 'Only a true artist could so arrange these delicate incisions (which are exceedingly slight) in so cunning a form as to be part of a well conceived and subtle decoration.' The incisions were incorporated into the design so that the less experienced paintresses at Wood's could place the design on to the wares with accuracy. It was noted that the long-established firm had updated its output with these designs, the keynote being 'modernity and simplicity'. Susie later went on to refine the 'Wren' shape for Wood's, resulting in the 'Jay' shape which did not have the incisions.

Falcon

'Falcon'-shaped wares, designed by Susie Cooper, appeared in early 1937 and covered a whole range of pottery. Cups without the shape's ribbed handles were produced for a short time; this model was known as 'Plain Falcon'. 'Falcon' was used extensively in the export markets.

Rex

This was a Wood's shape which Susie is supposed to have remodelled for her own use.

Classic

This was a Wood's shape which Susie probably remodelled for her own use. She began to use this shape over a limited range of wares in 1935.

Spiral

Designed by Susie Cooper, 'Spiral' was introduced in 1938, chiefly to tap into a more conservative, traditional market. The curved fluting of the wares did not lend itself readily to the lithographic process. It appears to have been used extensively for export, though Susie herself did not find the relatively ornate spiral shape particularly satisfying.

Quail

This bone china shape was introduced in 1951 and was used long after the introduction of its successor, the 'Can' shape.

Can

This bone china shape was introduced in 1958 and was used until the late 1980s at Wedgwood. The design was widely perceived as revolutionary and its longevity is a testament to its suitability for the application of decoration. Early coffee and tea pots and jugs have a 'body hugging' spout, which was later changed to a more traditional shape.

Fluted

The bone china 'Fluted' shape was a development of the 'Quail' shape. Introduced into Susie Cooper Productions in about 1956, the lightness of this ware is startling. Susie often used the 'Fluted' shape with minimal decoration, relying instead on the shape itself for aesthetic appeal.

The back stamps and markings illustrated below cover the entire working career of Susie Cooper and represent as complete a record as possible. New variations, however, may be found from time to time. Painted and incised signatures and markings (14 and 15, for instance) should not necessarily be assumed to be by Susie Cooper herself; indeed, few probably were, the majority being applied by her many paintresses.

Dates given for the back stamps can only be approximate; there is usually no record either of when a particular stamp came into use or when it was abandoned.

1 1912–28
Printed in black.
Variations: with pattern name; Gray's Pottery.

2 1921–31
Printed in black and yellow.
Variations: brown print;
Gray's Pottery;
pattern name included.

3 1923–31
Printed in blue or brown.
Variations: with 'Susie Cooper Nursery Ware';
pattern name included;
wavy line in place of 'Designed by Susie Cooper'.

4 1923–61
Printed in black and yellow.
Variations: gold or black print;
British Empire Exhibition 1924; with lion in black.

5 1931–61
Printed in green, yellow and black.
Variations: black print; Hanley England;
pattern name included.

6 1929
Rubber-stamped in black.
Variation: green or blue.

7 1930–32
Rubber-stamped in black.
Variation: outline around triangle.

8 1930–32
Rubber-stamped in black.
Variation: outline around triangle and words.

9 1932–34
Rubber-stamped in black.
Variations: pattern name included (e.g. 'The Homestead');
without line and 'BY'.

10 1932–34
Printed in black.

11 1932–64
Printed in browns.
Variations: green, pink, blue or black print;
reserve box (for pattern no.) included;
deer and 'A Susie Cooper Production' only;
pattern name (e.g. 'April') included.

12 1932–64
Printed in brown.
Variations: green or black print with pattern no.;
without reserve box;
with 'Susie Cooper' underlined and with circle.

13 1933–34
Wood's experimental translucent felspatic china body.

14 1930–80
Painted usually in black, brown, green or blue.
Many variations, since a number of paintresses would have painted the signature.

15 1932–92
Incised signature.
Many variations, since a number of paintresses would have carved the signature.

16 1932–34
Printed in black.
Variation: different pattern name.

17 1932–56
Printed in black.
Variations: blue print; without year (1932).

SHEPHERDS PURSE
BY

18 1932–34
Printed in black.

JOHN LEWIS
● POLKA DOTS

19 1934–58
Printed in black.
Variations: blue, green or orange print;
without pattern name.

DESIGNED BY

20 1935–c. 1942
Printed in black.
Variations: 'Designed by Susie Cooper for Awmacks, Leeds.
Manufactured by' above Wood and Sons Ltd.;
with pattern name 'Cavendish'.

Susie Cooper
ENGLAND.

21 1934–64
Printed in black.

Susie Cooper
England

22 1936–42
Printed in black. Variation: blue or brown print.

Susie Cooper
ENGLAND.
"DRESDEN"
1005

23 1936–60
Printed in black. Variations: without name and no.; different name and no.

"CHINESE BLUE"
JOHN LEWIS
AND
PETER JONES

24 1938–42
Printed in blue.

"MAHOGANY BAND"
MADE IN ENGLAND

25 1938–58
Printed in black. Variation: different pattern name.

Susie Cooper
England
Handpainted
· UNDERGLAZE ·
PERMANENT COLOURS
FERNDOWN
2374

26 1949–64
Printed in black. Variations: brown print; different pattern name and no.

Susie Cooper
✳
BONE CHINA
ENGLAND

27 1950–March 1966
Printed in brown. Variations: black, green or blue print; with pattern name and no.

Susie Cooper
CROWN WORKS
BURSLEM
ENGLAND
BLUE FERN
UNDERGLAZE HAND PAINTED
GUARANTEED
PERMANENT COLOURS
2377

28 1956–64
Printed in black. Variation: different pattern name and no.

SUSIE COOPER
ENGLAND
PARROT TULIP
E.2396

29 1960–64
Printed in red.

SUSIE COOPER
FINE
ENGLISH
BONE CHINA
MADE IN ENGLAND

30 1957–60
Printed in black.

Susie Cooper
SUSIE COOPER
FINE BONE CHINA
ENGLAND

31 1965–66
Printed in black. Variation: with pattern name and no.

Susie Cooper
SUSIE COOPER
FINE BONE CHINA
ENGLAND
Member of the
Wedgwood
Group

32 1967–68
Printed in black.

FINE BONE CHINA
Susie Cooper
MEMBER OF THE
WEDGWOOD GROUP
ENGLAND

33 1968–70
Printed in black.
Variation: with pattern name and no.

WEDGWOOD®
Bone China
Made in England
Susie Cooper Design

34 1969–88
Printed in black and gold. Variation: with pattern name.

Daisy

35 1982–c. 1986
Printed in blue or pink. Variation: without pattern name.

ADAMS®
Made in England

36 1982 onwards
Printed in black.

ADAMS®
MICRATEX®
COOKWARE
FOR FREEZER
COOKER MICROWAVE
TABLE AND
DISHWASHER
Made in England
Florida©

37 1982 onwards
Printed in black.
Variations: without pattern name;
with different name.

ADAMS
Susie Cooper
Design

38 1982 onwards
Printed in black.
Used experimentally.

PINK FERN©
ETRURIA
WEDGWOOD®
MADE IN
ENGLAND
BARLASTON
Susie Cooper Design

39 1987–88
Printed in black.
Variation: alternative pattern names to 'Pink Fern'.

GLOSSARY

(Including Susie Cooper's key decorative techniques)

Aerographed Colour is sprayed on to the pot either on or under the glaze. Susie Cooper is best known for her use of on-glaze aerographing, a useful technique for covering large areas.

Banding Traditionally used as a way of finishing off a design, Susie Cooper made banding the design itself. She used and developed this technique largely for reasons of economy; rather than holding many sizes of lithographs, a single motif could be applied in the centre of the design and the banding varied.

Banding wheel A wheel that is spun in order to apply a band of colour.

Biscuit Ceramic that is fired but unglazed.

Bone china Hard, translucent material which contains bone ash. Originally produced in the UK it is almost specific to this country.

Broken banding Used particularly in the early period of Susie Cooper's own factory, this technique involved banding in the normal way, with sections of the bands then wiped away.

Carving and incising A pot is taken in the 'leather hard' state (unfired and still drying out) and incisions made in the body. There is an almost limitless number of ways in which the clay can be marked. Susie Cooper quite often used an old screwdriver, the sharpened end of a brush, or a specially made metal point.

Coloured glazes Throughout her career Susie Cooper used the colour or texture of the glaze itself in the overall decorative effect of a pattern design.

Covercoat The printing technique used most commonly in the pottery industry today. Covercoat or 'slide' is produced by silk-screen printing on to collodion film. When the print is needed the paper is soaked, causing the design to slide off – hence the popular name, 'slide'. It is then put on to the ware. This technique has the advantage of being easier to handle than lithographic transfer printing.

Crayon In about 1932 Susie had the lumps of colour used for marking trials made into sticks. The crayon mark is applied on to biscuit ware and is therefore an under-glaze decoration. It can be used in virtually the same way as painted decoration.

Diaper A motif which is repeated at intervals over the surface of the pot.

Dontil A dash or spot made with a brush, usually on the edge or handles, to finish a design.

Earthenware The clay body which is low-firing and opaque.

Firing Biscuit firing is the heating of pottery in a kiln for the first time. Glost firing is the heating in a kiln of biscuit pottery that has been glazed.

Flat ware Plates, saucers, shallow dishes, etc.

Hollow ware Tea pots, coffee pots, jugs, cups, beakers, tureens, jam pots, etc.

In-glaze decoration This term refers to a large range of wares and is a technique that very much interested Susie Cooper. Under-glaze colours are painted on to a glazed pot and then fired to a high enough temperature for the colour to 'drop' into or fuse with the glaze. In the case of the painted studio wares, the design was painted on to the biscuit pot and then covered with cream glaze; the design and the body colour fused together when fired. In-glaze decoration tends to give depth and richness and also greater durability.

Kiln A device used to heat ceramics to make clay durable, sometimes referred to as an oven.

Lustre Metallic oxides in a medium applied as an on-glaze decoration; in firing the metal is deposited as a thin layer on the surface. The silver lustre most often used by Susie Cooper was in fact platinum suspended in medium, a relatively expensive decoration.

On-glaze enamel painting Enamels are produced by the grinding of coloured frits, or glazes. They are basically employed like conventional paint, with a single load of paint on a brush often used to create a motif. This speeded up the decorating process, but required great skills of precision and control. On-glaze enamels are fired at c. 750–800° C.

Pounce A method for copying a design. Tiny holes are pricked out of a piece of tissue paper to form a design; charcoal dust is then applied to the paper, transferring the design to the body of the ware.

Print and enamel Early printed decoration by Susie Cooper was created by the printing of an outline and the elaboration of the design using enamel decoration.

Reactive glaze Glaze which, when fired, gives a slightly different effect each time due to chemical reaction. Typically, the glaze gives multi-coloured or mottled effects.

Rubber stamping A rubber stamp is loaded with colour and pressed on to the surface of the pot.

Sculptural shapes Apart from the shapes of the table wares, Susie Cooper designed several sculptural and decorative three-dimensional works. The 'Walking Woman' figure, the table centres and the face masks were made into moulds for slip casting and were repeated for general sale.

Sgraffito This technique is particularly associated with aerographing but can be done in other kinds of decoration, such as banding. Sgraffito decoration involves scraping away a layer of colour, leaving the surface below to show through. There was a constant return to this technique throughout Susie Cooper's career, sometimes as a way of designing a printed pattern, e.g. 'Chou', 'Andromeda', etc. Sgraffito decoration, apart

from such obvious examples as sgraffito crescents, was sometimes used with extreme subtlety in Susie Cooper designs. Almost indiscernible brush strokes wipe away colour in, for example, the scrolls and stars design 1664.

Shaded banding Turpentine or other banding medium is applied to the surface of the glazed pot that is to be banded, then the pot is spun on a banding wheel and colour applied. As the colour on the brush runs out it gives the subtle effect of fading out.

Slip casting A method of mass-producing a clay object. Liquid clay (slip) is poured into a plaster mould; as the water is absorbed by the plaster, the clay takes on the moulded shape; when dry the object lifts away from the mould.

Solid banding This can be done on or under the glaze and literally refers to an opaque band of colour applied to the pot while it is spinning on the banding wheel.

Spiral banding This can be done on or under the glaze. Usually a large area of the pot is covered with the colour. Whilst banding, one side of the square-tipped brush is lifted off the surface leaving a subtle, lighter spiral through the colour.

Sponged decoration Because of its lack of sophistication, Susie Cooper used this technique only rarely.

String bands Thin bands of colour, often about $1/8$" wide.

Tracing The highlighting of such features as the edges of handles or spouts with a thin line.

Transfer printing Susie Cooper is credited with revolutionizing lithographic transfer printing. The technique involves printing designs on to paper which is then stuck down on to the ware with size (sticky potter's 'soap'). The paper is then moistened and peeled off, leaving the design ready to be fired at low enamel temperatures of approximately 750° C.

Tube-lining Liquid clay or colour is applied to the surface of the pot through a nozzle.

Tunnel oven Fires the ceramics on trolleys on a track through a long kiln in a 'conveyer belt'-like motion.

Under-glaze painting or decoration Applied to biscuit pottery. The key feature of this decoration is increased durability, as it is covered over by another layer of glaze, usually transparent.

Wash-banding On-glaze enamel colour that is increasingly thinned with turpentine or other banding medium to give successively more translucent colour bands.

White ware Ceramics that have been glazed but not decorated.

ACKNOWLEDGMENTS

During years of enthusiasm for the work of Susie Cooper and, more specifically, during the preparation of this book, many people have given me support, kindness and the use of their valuable time and facilities. My most heart-felt thanks, however, must be for the inspiration and encouragement which Susie Cooper herself offered me in the writing of the present work in the years before her death in 1995. The quotations from Susie Cooper in the main body of the book are taken from conversations held between Susie and myself during that period. This very personal thanks is also extended to her son, Tim Barker.

My parents and family, especially my research assistant Kath Youds.

The staff of the Wedgwood Museum for their invaluable help: Sharon Gater, Gaye Blake Roberts, Lynn Miller, Martin Chaplin, Sue Howdle and Joanne Riley. Peter Savill and Mike Poole of Nantwich Art Deco.
Nick Jones and Geoff Peake at Alfie's Antique Market, London. Jo Thackray and Susan Bennett of the R.S.A.

John Adams, Andy Andrews, Dave Bloor, Rosie Bowen Jones, Andrew Casey, Mrs. Marian Chainey, Joy and George Couper, Allison Dobbs, Christina Donaldson, Ann Eatwell, David and Ann Etchells, Ken and Doris Gleaves, Linda Izan, Waldemar Januczak, Barbara and Derek Morris, John Ryan, Susan Scott, Graham Stewart, Jenny, Martin and Janey Watson.

Argus Business Media, BBC Radio Stoke, Cinema and Theatre Association, *Designer* (published by SIAD, now the Chartered Society of Designers), Ellesborough Ltd., The Royal Society for the Encouragement of Arts, Manufacture and Commerce, Tableware International, Trustees of the Wedgwood Museum.